The Pocketbook of Audience Research

Focusing on qualitative methods, *The Pocketbook of Audience Research* uses contemporary, global television and cross-media examples to explain essential approaches to audience research and outline how they can be employed.

This handy guide is divided into three parts: the first part, 'Watching Post-Television', offers 'television' as a shortcut to understanding today's platform media and gives an introduction to key theoretical terms such as representation, identity and community. The second part, 'Methods with Method', introduces different methodological tools to study cross-media texts and practices from an audience-led perspective. With individual chapters covering ethnography, textual analysis and visual methodologies, this part also functions as a toolset and starting point for small research projects. The third part, 'Methods in Action', offers a variety of recent case studies to show how these methodological principles work in practice.

Drawing on different genres from drama to sports, *The Pocketbook of Audience Research* gives a sense of what audience-led cross-media research can achieve. This concise, accessible book gives students, early-career researchers and creative professionals the tools to do useful and inspiring audience research, whether for a paper, a proposal or a market survey.

Joke Hermes is a Dutch media and cultural studies researcher. She has published widely on popular culture, audience research and feminist analysis of gender and diversity. Currently, she is a Professor of Practice-based Research in Media, Culture and Citizenship at Inholland University; she teaches media studies at the University of Amsterdam. She was Founding Editor of the *European Journal of Cultural Studies*. Her most recent book is *Cultural Citizenship and Popular Culture: The Art of Listening.*

Linda Kopitz combines her professional experience as a creative director with her academic research on technology and everyday meaning-making. Her PhD research – situated between urban studies and media studies – explores the entanglement between real and virtual environments in sustainable architecture. As an interdisciplinary and practice-based scholar, she currently works as a Lecturer in Cross-Media Culture in Germany and The Netherlands. In parallel, she continues her professional work, with a specific focus on the sensory dimensions of communication.

The Pocketbook of Audience Research

Joke Hermes and Linda Kopitz

 Routledge
Taylor & Francis Group

LONDON AND NEW YORK

Designed cover image: Klaus Vedfelt / Getty

First published 2024
by Routledge
4 Park Square, Milton Park, Abingdon, Oxon OX14 4RN

and by Routledge
605 Third Avenue, New York, NY 10158

Routledge is an imprint of the Taylor & Francis Group, an informa business

© 2024 Joke Hermes and Linda Kopitz

British Library Cataloguing-in-Publication Data
A catalogue record for this book is available from the British Library

ISBN: 978-1-032-32513-2 (hbk)
ISBN: 978-1-032-32511-8 (pbk)
ISBN: 978-1-003-31542-1 (ebk)

DOI: 10.4324/9781003315421

Typeset in Sabon
by codeMantra

Contents

Acknowledgments   *vii*

Part I
Cross-media everyday meaning-making   1

Preamble: how to use this book   3

1 Introduction: audience research and the
   cross-media reality of post-television   6

2 Useful (key) theoretical terms:
   reconceptualizing audience research for
   deeply mediatized societies   19

Part II
**Methods with method: a methodic overview
of engaging with audiences**   33

3 Audience research: methods of data collection
   and data analysis need one another ♥   35

4 Ethnography
   Or: how to understand the value of presence   50
   WITH MARIAM YASSEIN

5 Audience-led analysis
   Or: on how to be invited 'in'   64

6 Visual analysis
   Or: how images and words 'mean' together   77

7 Theorization
   Or: how to get from data to theory   90

Part III
Case studies: methods in action   103

 8 Discourse analysis in practice: private attraction,
    public (dis)approval? Negotiating what to make
    of Netflix's *You*   105

 9 Data analysis in practice: data-scraping meets
    the Regency era: *Bridgerton* commentary on YouTube 119
    WITH CLAIR RICHARDS

10 Collaborative autoethnography in practice: "You
    knock on my door": an insider-outsider view of
    Turkish soap operas and fan labor   131

11 Media discourse analysis in practice:
    aren't we *Friends* anymore? Watching
    and rewatching the sitcom   141

12 Ethnography versus focus group research
    in practice: sports talk: watching, feeling and
    connecting   152

13 Visual analysis in practice: working through,
    laughing on: pandemic politics, cultural
    citizenship and action heroes   164

14 The long interview in practice: looking back:
    remembering favorite teen television shows   175
    WITH ERINN RÖVEKAMP

15 Afterthought: what's next?   188

    Index   191

Acknowledgments

To our brilliant students, past, present and future, for thinking about new challenges and new answers for audience research. We are specifically grateful to Clair Richards, Miriam Yassein and Erinn Rövekamp for allowing us to share their research projects with you in this book.

To our lovely colleagues, for encouraging us to write this book and offering nuanced comments about what needed to be in this book (or left out). We could not have done this without the insights of Toni Pape, Jan Teurlings, Markus Stauff, Jaap Kooijman, Marten Reesink and Misha Kavka.

To our fellow audience researchers, for challenging and changing the way research is thought and done. We would like to especially thank Ann Gray, Karel Koch, Annette Hill and Faye Mercier for sharing their approaches and experiences with us over the years.

To our wonderful editors Natalie Foster and Kelly O'Brien at Routledge, for their patience and care in turning an open idea into a material – and hopefully useful – book. And of course to our anonymous peer reviewers for helping us in connecting the last open strands.

To our informants, participants and interviewees, for allowing us to see the world through your eyes and with your help. Both online and offline, for brief moments or via long conversations.

To our readers, for allowing us to introduce you to audience research in and through the lens of cross-media practices and realities. We are looking forward to your feedback and can't wait to see how you make these methods your own.

Part I

Cross-media everyday meaning-making

Preamble
How to use this book

The Pocketbook of Audience Research takes as its starting point that we are all audiences and that being an audience can take many forms. Those forms include that as audiences we use media ritually and without paying them much mind but that we are also producers: texts of whatever audiovisual, aural or written kind (a song, a television program, a book, a newspaper) need us to make them meaningful. In addition, we might talk or tweet about them and use them to make a response video or a meme. Audience research therefore takes many forms. Audiences can be studied by talking with them (in individual interviews or in focus groups). As audiences are also media makers, there is a range of forms of media content and cultural artifacts produced by audiences that are of interest. Think of tweets, online content but also of collages made in creative design research. Then, third, there are all kinds of data that can add to audience analysis. Numbers of viewers, subscribers, likes, retweets, comments, as well as the media objects themselves all can help provide a better sense of how we are audiences and how audiencehood affords us a crucial link to one another and to both formal and informal institutions in today's thoroughly mediated societies.

All of these different sources of information help make clear what is produced in audiencehood and how being an audience member is meaningful in its own right (it may help build a sense of identity, check what is 'normal', organize domestic life or allow for a conversation about most any topic). Often, research projects touch on different layers of knowledge (knowledge coming from direct exchange, knowledge through what audience members have said and made and the data collected about them by the owners of online platforms but also by, e.g., broadcasting institutions). Here, we have tried to keep them apart to show the individual strengths of different methods that might be used. Do know that using methods across these layers can be a good way of 'triangulating' what you find. By comparing outcomes of different methods, different perspectives can unfold on what you are interested in and

DOI: 10.4324/9781003315421-3

deepen your understanding. A well-triangulated (bigger) project can also be more convincing to its readers and users.

While moving across different layers of knowledge and meaning-making, we have chosen not to try to include the widest possible range of media or of all possible genres. Instead, television provides a lens and focus point that radiates out across a broad cross-media intertextual web. Chapter 1 will clarify how we understand 'television' in an era of platform media and why it has been given pride of place in a book that invites you to engage with audience research far more broadly. *The Pocketbook of Audience Studies* consists of three distinctive parts. The chapters can be read individually and in whatever order pleases the reader.

The first part "Cross-Media Everyday Meaning-Making" offers a definition of why 'television' makes for an easy and accessible example in an era of platform media for those wanting to be informed about how to do audience research. It also offers an introduction to key theoretical terms. The chapter introduces qualitative audience research in relation to television as a way to understand how an audience-led 'critique' of media culture can help understand broader logics of culture and of mediation or how we relate to the world through media. Chapter 2 offers key theoretical terms that return in audience research as it has been written up by academics in media and cultural studies. An example of the importance of being familiar with such terms is for instance in how we see 'people' not as individual persons but in terms of identities and subjectivity. It will allow us to move from conversations with individuals (that all of us engage in) to broader questions of cultural logic and social power. Then there are terms that have to do with research. They define what it is we are looking for and what it is that we '(re)construct': frames, discourses, repertoires.

The second part "Methods with Method: A Methodic Overview of Engaging with Audiences" introduces different methodological tools. They all belong under the broad umbrella of 'media ethnography'. (The remit of ethnography and media ethnography as both descriptive and interpretative qualitative research will be introduced in Part I.) With individual chapters covering ethnography (Chapter 4), audience-led analysis (Chapter 5), visual analysis (Chapter 6) and theorizing data (Chapter 7), this part functions as a toolset and starting point for case study projects that function as examples. Each of the chapters in this part of the book will also present shorter examples to offer a sense of how the methods described there can be applied to (small) research projects.

The third part of the book, "Case Studies: Methods in Action", offers a variety of recent 'stand alone' case studies to see how the methodological principles presented in Part II, work in practice. They draw on different genres from the serial killer drama *You* (Chapter 8), reaction videos to the Regency romance series *Bridgerton* on YouTube (Chapter 9), Turkish soap operas (Chapter 10), mediated discourses of the sitcom *Friends* (Chapter 11), memes about the news during the Covid-19 pandemic (Chapter 13), to live and mediated sports (Chapter 12) and memories of teen television (Chapter 14). It will become clear that an audience-led perspective offers a wealth of possibilities.

1 Introduction

Audience research and the cross-media reality of post-television

There are a great many books about audience research: some address general principles, some focus on television, social media and other forms of media culture. But there are not so many that introduce *doing* audience research. **This one will.** Not as a lengthy tome, but as a handy pocketbook that you will be able to go back to throughout your academic life as a student and your post-academic life outside of the university. With a focus on qualitative methods, this pocketbook is also meant for (young) professionals – should you be so happy as to find a research job in the media, the advertising or marketing industry or in higher education. *The Pocketbook of Audience Research* will explain essential approaches and outline how they can be employed. The methodological umbrella term that we will use for those different approaches is media ethnography. The many tools that media ethnography offers are useful for any kind of qualitative (audience) research project. Our starting point for this exploration of everyday meaning-making with and through media is television. Before you roll your eyes at this: we like television and think that despite several major crises, something we call 'television' will be with us for the foreseeable future. We hope that while reading this book, you will find that television is not only this 'old' medium – but that it is also deeply connected to other forms of contemporary social and print media culture. 'Television' can be different things, depending on whether you think about the device, the makers, the audience or the content. It's an accessible example and a good reference point. Television, in all its different forms from reality shows via news broadcasting to serial drama, travels across contexts and platforms. Its definition shifts and changes depending on who you are talking to. *The Pocketbook of Audience Research* will use contemporary, global examples of cross-media texts and how these are present on and via different (social) media platforms in everyday life.

To use television for a book about audience research would have been a strange thing to suggest 12 years or even one decade ago. Around the millennium change, television was expected to become a medium of

DOI: 10.4324/9781003315421-3

the past and disappear in favor of new platform-based forms of screen entertainment and information. Indeed, about a decade and a half ago, audience researchers, too, were seeing that 'television' had become a problematic category. When we asked people about watching television, they would be confused: what exactly did we mean? In the mid-2010s, television had lost part of its easy-to-recognize technological 'form'. Hence, the questions: unprogrammed content, is that television? Something you watch on a computer, does that count? Did we mean Netflix? Or the longer segments on YouTube? Vertical entertainment (watching television and continuing on a program-related app or on to social media platforms to vent frustration or share excitement)? As will become clear: we mean all of the above.

'Television': a ridiculously short history

For a brief moment in time, during the Covid pandemic in 2020–2022, television (perhaps even more than other media) became a lifeline. With nostalgic abandon older and younger viewers returned to all forms of television: linear, platform library, time-lapsed, pay-on-demand. Watching press conferences live or re-watching old favorites, television offered 'comfort' in a disrupted time. This somewhat surprising discovery suggests that 'television' as a medium and as a term is good to go for at least another decade, now on a multitude of devices. Historically, television had been a linear and limited broadcast medium that from the mid-twentieth century onward delivered content via a small number of channels at set times. Programming meant that television dictated when it could be viewed. To be able to do that, to get audiences to structure their day around a set schedule, television won its audiences by offering access to events one would want to be present at – but could not. Often-quoted is Queen Elizabeth II's coronation in 1953. Equally important examples of early television include sports matches. Indeed, Philips, the Dutch global producer of television sets in the twentieth century, built a soccer stadium in 1910 for its personnel sports society. The Philips team would later become PSV, a European major league club. Unsurprisingly, the stadium was used for test transmissions shortly after the Second World War.

Soap opera, quiz and game shows (in the United States), news, sports and situation comedies (almost everywhere) did the work of further enamoring entire nations of the 'box'. This is not a metaphor: programmed television came out of a clunky, box-shaped object that found its space in living rooms aided by advertising campaigns in women's magazines that instructed readers as to where it should be positioned (Spigel 1992). More than half a century later, from the 1990s and early 2000s onward, 'television' comes out of online 'libraries' and personal recording devices, or, more and more rarely, from DVD's. Programming became flexible: delayed viewing stopped requiring recording (with the right kind of subscription to a cable company). Flat screens, computers, phones, wall projection: they all deliver home information and entertainment. Jumping another two decades, smart televisions communicate with telephones and laptop computers. Cross-media content, ranging from news and current affairs programs to reality television, movies, quiz shows and signature drama have become an interlinked media reality.

Television audience research has been important for theorizing 'television' in media and cultural studies: a couple of examples

Raymond Williams published a ground-breaking study about television in 1974 that included autoethnographic reflection. He introduces 'mobile privatization' and 'flow' as key terms. Although television gives us a far broader knowledge of the world, extending far beyond where we live, it also ties us to our homes. Flow, in addition, is how Williams first described the way television (and now social media) keep us locked to the screen.

Television, says John Hartley in *Uses of Television*, is a neighborly medium, and it introduces us to distant others as if they were just around the corner (1999). He draws on informal examples.

According to Roger Silverstone, media offer audiences ontological security: a stable sense of being (1994, 5–8). He worked with David Morley (1986), who conducted extensive research with media users that also spoke to family power relations.

According to Annette Hill, who has done extensive audience research on news and nonfiction genres such as reality television, media allow us to 'roam'. Even when audiences choose from what is on offer, there is a sense in which they roam texts and platforms (Hill 2019). Sometimes they roam following established pathways in national settings and do 'broadcast tv'. When using streaming television, sharing content, and reacting to it in Reddit threads, audiences follow their own paths. Roaming can also be pathmaking when viewers make their own content, distribute it through social media, or on YouTube, and react to such user-generated content in Twitter feeds. As pathmakers, roamers become both producers and audiences, co-creating new forms of television and televisual flow.

Television is a platform for cultural citizenship, argues Joke Hermes (2005) on the basis of a series of small audience research projects. Well before social media arrived, television established itself as a supplier of material to talk about (within and outside of your immediate circle of family, friends and acquaintances) and have authoritative feelings about. It is a space in which to think about, reflect on and (re)form identities that are embedded in communities of different kinds, both existing in real life and virtually.

Implied in our use of television are processes of distinction and rule-making: ethical norms as much as aesthetic evaluation and assessments of truth and sincerity of others, Skeggs and Wood found in their research on reality television with women from different class backgrounds (2012). It is a process of bonding and community building and reflection on that bonding.

Speaking of entertainment: new genres have been added to television throughout its history – but not at the speed one would expect. As with the shift from programmed to scheduled viewing, they were also connected to technological shifts. Reality television was an innovation of the 1990s made possible by new high-definition video technology which allowed for split screens and inserts (Caldwell 1995). Without those, reality television would have offered content too deeply boring to capture large audiences. Quality television, as a separate category of drama, also depended on superior technology becoming available. Even more, it was a means, in a changing television landscape, for television broadcasters to distinguish themselves (McCabe and Akass 2007). It might seem that the end of the twentieth century offered more excitement in terms of content than the new Millennium has done so far. Not that much seems to have changed in the types of content that are produced, apart from more 'male melodrama' and sports chat shows (Mittell 2015). Multimedia formats have been developed that include games and social media to work in tandem with programmed television. However, there are other changes that are fascinating to follow – especially as it comes to an increasingly globalized and interconnected media landscape. Much of the television literature focuses on the American market. In earlier decades, the British BBC would have been focused on as the gold standard for quality television production. In the mid-2000s, South-Korean television became one of the most interesting to follow for its innovation, cross-mediated star system and enormous global reach of audiences (Chua and Iwabuchi 2008). Given Nigeria's formidable film industry, often referred to as 'Nollywood', this is also a region to watch for new forms and formats in television production.

If anything, it is audiences themselves who have revolutionized television viewing these past years. Their extended practices of cross-media use are what interest us here, while we salute how remarkably stable 'television' is in its storytelling. Today, streaming platforms have found their way into our everyday life: projected onto the 'television' screen in living rooms, on laptops and tablets and other secondary devices such as phones. Moving away from both the 'schedule' and the 'box', 'television' has again become the term that is used widely for a particular type of visual storytelling. Of course, some of what made television viewing stand out as a media practice has taken on different forms in today's 'post-television' era. From shared viewing experience to the discussion of what's 'on': they will now likely involve other media platforms as well as individual stories in addition to household ones. We google what to watch, act on a Whatsapp conversation with a friend, a YouTube response video or an online newspaper review. We watch audio-visual content created by ourselves and by others. The more professional the production and the bigger the screen, the more likely it is that you will call it 'watching tv'. But, as this book suggests, all our media use these days has become a cross-media practice that involves more platforms. If not in the moment, then at some point in the near or slightly further away future.

In media studies, this simultaneous expansion of audience practices, content production and technological infrastructures is referred to as 'cross-media' or even 'trans-media' to highlight the multiple relationships between us and our screen(s). Some of the experiences and practices are dependent on technological infrastructures and access points; some of them extend through and across them. This is precisely why we are using 'television' as our starting point here: to trace how we make meaning in and through media, in a changing media landscape.

Television audience research, disrupted: a case of a disappearing research object

It will have been a drama for the researchers, but there is also a kind of irony in how history (in this case disguised as Netflix) can trick a well-designed project. After having become a household staple with a 60-year history, 'television' briefly disappeared from the radar of audiences in the 2010s. A large Australian research project was virtually derailed by the arrival of online platform-based television. The goal of the project was to investigate cultural consumption in a range of cultural 'fields' – literature, music, visual arts, sport, heritage and television. A questionnaire was administered by telephone to a sample of 1,400 people about their habits of consumption. The questions were based on the assumption that television equaled 'broadcast television' as it was established in the second half of the last century. Thoughtfully, the design included 45 follow-up interviews with individuals so that they could elaborate on their answers regarding television. Elaborate they did, to such an extent that the television questions from the questionnaire lost their value. Interviewees simply did not connect their new Netflix viewing with 'television'. With Netflix, apparently, a new mode of television viewing had come into being. Graeme Turner (2019), who wrote about this project, suggests that we need to research 'cultures of use'. We know about the industry, about texts but what do we know about practices of media audiencehood, he asks? Given how deeply television viewing (watching a screen for often-serialized audio-visual content that entertains and/or informs) is embedded in everyday routines, (cross-) media ethnography is a most promising route to understand audiencehood in its own right.

Other authors who have written about the coming of 'internet-distributed television' and 'online television' are Cathy Johnson (2019), Amanda Lotz (2018 and 2022) and Mareike Jenner (2018, 2021).

Television, media ethnography and storytelling

'Television' is not only connected to specific forms of 'sociality' (watching together), but televisual storytelling also has two interesting distinctive characteristics. From its very early years on, television has favored *never-ending stories*, whether in entertainment or in news formats. The genre known as 'the soap opera' is generally seen as defining television (Newcomb 2007). It took time for what was initially seen as 'mere' melodrama to spread out from the soap series. Today, we see how television has continued to spin out themes and storylines by introducing us to *returning key characters* (whether celebrities, presenters, pop and sports stars, political or fictional figures). It offers us a sense of being part of its extended families. In terms of sociality, television's winning trait is in how it provides for home entertainment and information. It allows us *to be together with others without having to talk, or by offering things to talk about*: a win-win medium offering a 360 degree of choices in whether and how to be with others. Although television was briefly threatened by new forms of audio-visual entertainment and information, platform television managed to regain its place in the living room via the smart television and its even smarter remote control. As a central information and entertainment 'hub', television is expected to be a key media space for the coming decades (Hermes and Hill 2020). That makes being able to do cross-media television audience research a useful competence and starting point for audience research generally.

How to research televisual storytelling and the storytelling that television, in turn, gives rise to?

Posing the question like this suggests that textual analysis and audience research do very different things. However, as audience researchers are also television viewers, it can be extremely useful to include textual analysis in audience research as a form of reflection on one's own viewing experience and those of others. Methodologically, such reflection can be part of autoethnographic research – which can then be extended into collaborative (auto)ethnography. Or, it can be a good way for you as a researcher to not be caught up in your own preconceived notions. Bringing preconceptions to the surface makes it easier to listen to others and to hear what they are saying, which brings us to our next important point: method.

Old methods for new practices and new methods for old practices

The Pocketbook of Audience Studies uses media ethnography as a blanket term to cover different forms of qualitative research. Different kinds of interviewing, of observing others, of attending to texts are discussed and used: all of these tools have been available for a long time.

- The humanities and philosophy have offered ways to understand the world, how we are in it, how we know what we know. It teaches us to respect context and locality. The place we see the world from matters, as do the lifeworlds of the audiences we study
- The social sciences, such as sociology and anthropology, developed a great many tools for qualitative research. So-called grounded theory research, as developed by Glaser and Strauss in the 1960s is the basis for a very doable and effective form of analysis of audience materials. It is presented in Chapter 2

- Cultural studies, as developed from the late 1970s onward, offered the kind of media ethnography that is also promoted here. It is an approach that is interested in everyday-meaning making while paying attention to the power relations that shape, among other things, practices of media use
- This means that we are using old methods to approach a new world. When media ethnography was developed as a method, social media did not exist. As we shall see, these old methods work well enough with new viewing practices, especially when we combine the old methods for media texts and practices, with new methods for old (and new) media. New methods are, for instance, scraper tools such as Coosto, video call software that allows for immediate transcription, or the qualitative data analysis software that helps code and interpret large data sets.

The power of the old methods is that they teach that meaning is always constructed and never 'just there'. Media ethnography attends to meaning-making *in action*. With today's new media, we often feel very close to meaning-making as it happens. Think of how Twitter (now X) can 'explode' with outrage over media representation. Don't be fooled into thinking such meaning-making is a different beast than the old-fashioned television viewing that informants talk about in interviews. On Twitter (or X), as in interviews, people perform: they use the affordances of the platform and their own cultural knowledge to show themselves to be funny and smart in a limited number of characters (and now images). We see meaning-making performed on X, much as it is performed (though perhaps less obviously) elsewhere. And yes, the old methods work pretty well in making sense of meaning-making on new media platforms. Just as the new methods are a great help in exploring how audiences love and hate 'old' media – if only by giving us faster access to much larger repositories of discussion where we can enjoy being unobtrusive, or if we wish, participant observers.

Media ethnography has a respectable history as a qualitative research method in media and cultural studies. We will use it as the general label for the research presented and explained in this book. Ethnography originally is the method of anthropologists. It means: describing (graphein in Greek) other people (ethnos, a people). In autoethnography, you make yourself the object of your observations to interpret patterns, habits and processes of meaning-making. (Auto means 'self' in classic Greek). A small step really to full textual research which uses the methods of literary theorists and pays attention to narrative, to characters or to aesthetics. Following the development of collective, mediated storytelling informs us about how societies change. Paying precise and explicit attention to, for instance, television texts is valuable as it can tell us about identity and representation and collective norms for behavior and looks. When textual research becomes 'audience-led', it gains in value. Rather than understand texts as 'influencing' us, we start to see how we take texts up in meaning-making. Rather than decide for others how television's texts are important, a television audience researcher will more humbly start from what others like (or hate, or find important) in their television viewing. They will find the techniques of literary theorists or film scholars useful to give depth to the study of how practices of cross-media use are made sense of in everyday life.

The way television tells stories

In an early television studies book, Fiske and Hartley (1978) describe television as the 'bard of our times'. John Ellis (2000) has noted that television is more than a storyteller. It helps us 'work through' the anxieties of our time. Television has been able to do this because its storytelling is open-ended and seeks syntagmatic rather than paradigmatic complexity and, thus, works well across breaks. These terms come from early work on television by Newcomb (1974) and Allen (1987). Both refer to soap opera as the type of program that distinguishes television from other media. Soap opera's logic of storytelling has permeated television's storytelling. A famous example is the cop show (or police series). From linear narratives about bringing perpetrators to justice (that follow a 'paradigmatic' logic), they have become multistoryline tales with large casts of characters that we follow across their personal and professional lives (a syntagmatic logic) (Johnson 2006).

Like the extended family of the nineteenth and early twentieth century, the 'work families' of 'soapified' drama series promised to never completely fall apart. Syntagmatic storytelling circles and repeats, building a unique type of suspense while allowing for a viewer to miss large chunks of a program and still be able to make sense of the narrative. What happened will be repeated when the focus shifts to another character. The large casts of soaps also offer the possibility of multiple perspectives on any given event that we witness through concurrent narratives (Brunsdon 1997, 15).

Rather than (only) follow the storyline, or paradigmatic narrative logic, we learn to enjoy syntagmatic complexity and comparing viewpoints. This following of multiple perspectives opens up the private lives of others for us to take an (imaginary) part in.

Some key considerations: citizenship, belonging, technology

Across the history of media, citizenship is important. Citizenship is basically how we belong in and to nation-states and how that gives us both rights and duties. Such a broad social contract needs a common language but also a sense of a shared history and a shared culture. Television, like radio before it, in addition, offers national news programs that provide citizens with the means to exert their citizenship well. In audience research, we often find that 'belonging' is important. 'Identity' (to have a sense of who you are in relation to others and of how others see you) and 'representation' are concepts that are often used in the literature and that will be further discussed in relation to audience research in Chapter 2. Cultural citizenship is another such term that is important: it is discussed further in several chapters. It refers to how media and popular culture allow us to connect to others (and, thus, to belong) by sharing thoughts and ideas about the world in conversation about what we have seen. Herein too lies the importance of being able to do audience research. It is less a matter of understanding how media influence individual people (which is a question we leave to psychologists) as a question of how people shape their worlds with the help of media and how media are important to them.

The link of media use to the nation-state also attends us to the contexts in which media operate. Nation-states are in charge of law and order, as part of which they will regulate media. In the good sense, and the bad sense. Where there is strong public broadcasting, rampant commercialism will be forbidden, as is the case in most European countries. Where there is a strong entrepreneurial ethic, media makers and broadcasters will be forbidden to become too big and monopolize industries, as is the case in, e.g., the United States. Audience researchers try to be aware of such political-economic questions. After all, to media users, advertising makes an enormous difference. Most of us are hardly indifferent to breaks in programs. Whether we hate ads, have to laugh at them or are irritated by them, they are part of how media use is made meaning of.

Another relevant context to media use this book will not particularly focus on, is media technology. There is a long intellectual history of thinking through how particular technological forms will drive practices of use and meaning-making. Such technologies can be part of the making or consuming of media content, think of the high-definition video revolution toward the end of the last century (Caldwell 1995). It allowed for faster television production, for higher quality standards and for entirely new genres. As part of the change from analog to digital technology, it also meant changes in the machines audiences could use for storing and playback of content. Around such technological innovations and changes, there tend to be happy expectations of a better, more convenient, more fun and more equal world. There are almost always also fears. Media and media technology will steer us in directions we may not have wanted to go in. The important point for audience research is to ask people about this and to understand that common sense notions may make viewers and users hesitant. At the crossroads of science and technology studies and media studies, interesting examples can be found of how new technologies in other fields are pioneered via, e.g., television. For the sports-minded, Carlos d'Andréa and Markus Stauff (2022) offer a fascinating discussion of how the introduction of the video referee in football was negotiated by football fans on Twitter.

Engaging with audiences also comes with ethical responsibilities. We need to ask those whose practices we study for consent. Informants and those we observe need to be treated with respect, regardless of their opinions or behavior. In qualitative audience research, we do not concern ourselves with individuals, with what they say or do or with the effects of media consumption on their behavior. We are interested in *culture*: how it is built and maintained. Meaning-making is always a collective process that uses shared resources. Those resources are available as shared stories or interpretative frames, as ways to understand the world. Of course we can be critical of the stories, of how they exclude or offend. When we are, it is imperative that we do not conflate what people say with what they are. Audience researchers are cultural critics who are invested in listening well and to opening up conversation. We are not the police of taste or of morality. We are aware that we toe a line. In our work, we represent others, over which those we represent mostly have little control. It is your choice what to do with your audience research. It can be used to refine campaigns or products. It can also be used to enrich public discussion or aid the emancipation of vulnerable others.

References

Andréa, Carlos d', and Markus Stauff. 2022. "Mediatized Engagements with Technologies: 'Reviewing' the Video Assistant Referee at the 2018 World Cup." *Communication & Sport* 10 (5): 830–53. https://doi.org/10.1177/21674795221076882.

Allen, Robert. 1987. *Channels of Discourse: Television and Contemporary Criticism.* 1st ed. Chapel Hill: University of North Carolina Press.

Brunsdon, Charlotte. 1997. *Screen Tastes: Soap Opera to Satellite Dishes.* London/New York: Routledge.

Caldwell, John Thornton. 1995. *Televisuality: Style, Crisis, and Authority in American Television.* Communication, Media, and Culture. New Brunswick, NJ: Rutgers University Press.

Chua, Beng Huat, and Kōichi Iwabuchi, eds. 2008. *East Asian Pop Culture: Analysing the Korean Wave.* Hong Kong/London: Hong Kong University Press/Eurospan [distributor].

Ellis, John. 2000. *Seeing Things: Television in the Age of Uncertainty.* London/New York: I.B. Tauris.

Fiske, John, and John Hartley. 1978. *Reading Television.* New Accents. London: Methuen.

Hartley, John. 1999. *Uses of Television.* London/New York: Routledge.

Hermes, Joke. 2005. *Rereading Popular Culture.* Cambridge: Blackwell.

Hermes, Joke, and Annette Hill. 2020. "Television's Undoing of Social Distancing." *European Journal of Cultural Studies* 23 (4): 655–61. https://doi.org/10.1177/1367549420927724.

Hill, Annette. 2019. *Media Experiences: Engaging with Drama and Reality Television.* London/New York: Routledge.

Jenner, Mareike. 2018. *Netflix and the Re-Invention of Television.* 1st ed. Cham: Springer International Publishing/Imprint/Palgrave Macmillan. https://doi.org/10.1007/978-3-319-94316-9.

———, ed. 2021. *Binge-Watching and Contemporary Television Studies.* Edinburgh: Edinburgh University Press.

Johnson, Catherine. 2019. *Online Television.* London/New York: Routledge.

Johnson, Steven. 2006. *Everything Bad Is Good for You: How Today's Popular Culture Is Actually Making Us Smarter.* 1st Riverhead trade pbk. ed. New York: Riverhead Books.

Lotz, Amanda D. 2022. *Netflix and Streaming Video: The Business of Subscriber-Funded Video on Demand.* Cambridge/Medford, MA: Polity Press.

Lotz, Amanda D. 2018. *We Now Disrupt This Broadcast: How Cable Transformed Television and the Internet Revolutionized It All.* Cambridge, MA: The MIT Press.

Mittell, Jason. 2015. *Complex TV: The Poetics of Contemporary Television Storytelling.* New York: New York University Press.

Morley, David. 1986. *Family Television: Cultural Power and Domestic Leisure.* Comedia Series, no. 37. London: Comedia Pub. Group.

Newcomb, Horace. 1974. *TV: The Most Popular Art.* 1st ed. Garden City, NY: Anchor Press.

———, ed. 2007. *Television: The Critical View.* 7th ed. New York: Oxford University Press.

Silverstone, Roger. 1994. *Television and Everyday Life.* London/New York: Routledge.

Skeggs, Beverley, and Helen Wood. 2012. *Reacting to Reality Television: Performance, Audience and Value.* New York: Routledge.

Spigel, Lynn. 1992. *Make Room for TV: Television and the Family Ideal in Postwar America*. Chicago: University of Chicago Press.

Turner, Graeme. 2019. "Approaching the Cultures of Use: Netflix, Disruption and the Audience." *Critical Studies in Television: The International Journal of Television Studies* 14 (2): 222–32. https://doi.org/10.1177/1749602019834554.

Williams, Raymond. 1974. *Television: Technology and Cultural Form*. Technosphere. London: Fontana.

2 Useful (key) theoretical terms

Reconceptualizing audience research for deeply mediatized societies

This chapter introduces you to (some of) the central concepts of cross-media audience research. They are linked to examples to show what kind of storytelling research allows for. Storytelling is a form of theorization – of finding narrative logic based on the combination of concepts, questions and the interpretation of collected data. In other words, audience research allows us to do complex jigsaw puzzles that help understand the narratives that are shared in contemporary deeply mediatized societies, the social rules and mechanisms that are embodied in these narratives and our feelings about them.

The three sets of terms in this chapter focus on (1) **the individual**, (2) **shared culture** and (3) **methodology**. In qualitative audience research, we often work with individuals or small groups of people – but we are interested in culture as a *shared* accomplishment. Culture needs us as individuals to continue to exist but is also something that no individual controls on their own. In fact, in many ways, culture controls us. An example would be norms for how to behave or look. The second set of terms focuses on the social level at which media operate. It clarifies why qualitative audience research identifies *practices* in relation to structures of meaning-making. Taste is a good example. It would seem to be something a person has. It turns out that taste is not something you have but an acquired set of norms and standards that we rely on in finding our way in life: taste is how we navigate what art to like, how to dress and behave the right way. Taste helps distinguish ourselves from others. Ultimately, taste does not define a person but the groups to which you want (or do not want) to belong. The key author here is Pierre Bourdieu (1984). The third set of terms has to do with how methodology is a craft that comes with specific tools. Some of those have already made their way into Chapter 1 and even in this chapter. When meaning-making is presented as a practice, it means that meaning is never given but comes into being under specific power relations (to do with class, gender, ethnicity, religion and so on) and, therefore, needs deconstruction as a

DOI: 10.4324/9781003315421-4

critical practice. Deconstruction in the context of this book is both a philosophical *and* a methodological point of departure.

First level: from the individual to the subject

It is not necessary to adhere to post-structuralist insights to do qualitative audience research. It does make it easier to do it well when you understand the basic tenets of such an approach. When we speak of individuals, there is a suggestion of boundaries. The skin and the body's mucous membranes are where a person ends and the world begins. Inside the body, it is easy to imagine a mind and a will that make that body act and reflect. Thinking in such a way is to understand individuals as autonomous beings. It is clear that autonomy is at the very least, in part, an illusion. Acting in the world requires language (which precedes us, it exists long before we are born) and knowledge of how to behave. Those are per definition shared.

Sociologists, anthropologists, researchers thinking about language suggest that partly we have '**agency**', a measure of control, when it comes to language. Partly, we do not. You may be familiar with semiotics as defined by Ferdinand de Saussure in the early twentieth century. He posits that there is a difference between 'langue' (French for language as a formal system) and 'parole' (talk, or language as spoken). Because we use formal systems, they will change. We make mistakes or we try to change things which results in new codes. As times change, new words and meanings are needed. Those that are less and less used slip away.

Roland Barthes on myth

In the 1957 book called *Mythologies* (translated into English in 1972), Roland Barthes explains how the distance between a word as sound, or a set of letters and what it means, offers space for ideology to come into being. If language is simply a set of codes and social conventions, nothing much is the matter. After all, we can situate those codes and conventions historically and understand where they come from. That tells us, for instance, what interests and power relations they are connected with. Words, however, can themselves become mere basic material for what he calls 'second order signification'. When we lose where words come from, they can achieve mythic status. They simply become a given and suggest that what the world is like, is its 'natural' state. This, Barthes calls mythology. Others speak of ideology, a shared worldview that hides power inequality and tells us what our place (and the place of others) is in it. By disavowing their history and appearing as 'natural,' ideologies can help condone insidious forms of social inequality that are, for instance, racist, sexist or transphobic. Do read the 'Myth Today' essay in Roland Barthes' book (1972). For examples of how audience research can benefit from Barthes work, read Annette Hill's book *Media Experiences* (2019).

When we think of the autonomous individual in this light, she is, in many ways, defined by the language that is at her disposal. She speaks – but not with means she developed on her own or for herself. Instead of thinking about persons as individuals, it is useful to think about them as 'subjects'. The French philosopher, historian and activist Michel Foucault (1926–1984) offers '**subjectivity**' as consisting of two parts: the one half is about how we are 'subjected' to systems such as language (but also state control), and the other half is that we feel we are 'subjects' in the sense that the world turns around us. The subject in grammar is the central element of a sentence. Individuality is the product of such a perspective. Foucault takes this further and shows how we are not only disciplined to become individuals but that we take pleasure in being part of our own subjectification. A concept you may come across in relation to this is '**governmentality**'.

Governmentality addresses precisely how '**power**' works as a peculiar kind of pressure to fall in line. It is how states (from the bureaucracy to the police and the military) govern populations by aiming to influence individual behavior. Governments in the Global North do not so much discipline people (although they do have that option through the state power of the police, the military and the legal system) but rely in large part on their willing participation. The media are important here, and they offer examples (of what is and is not okay, what we should aspire to) and incentives. Deconstruction of practices of meaning-making needs to always also address how these examples are entangled with disciplinary power and with the neoliberal ideology they back up. While neoliberalism with its focus on individuals and individuality pleasantly suggests autonomy and that we are the architects of our own success, it is a horrible frame for those who are not wealthy or find themselves on the wrong side of any number of good-bad dichotomies that underlay definitions of gender, race and ethnicity, sexuality or ability. Not having success, being poor, not fitting in, being discriminated against, bullied, excluded are defined as personal faults. It is how the social power dynamics that are instigated by states (to classify individuals by income, profession, living arrangement, race) are masked and perpetuated. In all cases, attending to how social power relations are acknowledged or disavowed will afford better insight in everyday processes of meaning-making. We are not 'controlled' by the media but by states that identify, classify, order and control us.

A good example in audience research is when interviewees speak of 'guilty pleasures'. That sounds as much of a paradox as the Foucault-based explanation of subjectivity above. Usually, guilty pleasure refers to enjoying television programs or movies that are deemed to be in 'bad taste'. They are overly melodramatic or not well-made. The term does not seem to apply to social media use. In that case informants say: I am addicted. Addiction is the superlative of guilty pleasure. It is taking pleasure beyond the boundaries of what is healthy. Neither is 'true'. Most of the guilty pleasure 'bad taste' examples are innocent and reflect the other person's upbringing or what they think the interviewer will or will not like to hear. Addiction also is hardly meant in a clinical sense. There is no deep wish to detox. Rather, it appears to intensify the pleasure of gaming or checking in on social media to suggest that it is a bit dangerous. These two examples suggest that as 'subjects' we enjoy the distance between being subjected to rules and norms while we also feel their weight and their supposed rationality. In referring to them and abiding by them, we strengthen the very norms and rules that we also seek to be free from.

Psychology and the individual

Psychologists have a very different way of looking at individuals and personhood. As a discipline, psychology is deeply invested in therapy and helping individuals feel better, work through their mental health problems and stay away from what harms them. In media research, psychologists have worked with experiments to test how for instance mediated violence is harmful to children. Harmful here means that they become anxious or violent and display behavior that bothers or hurts others. The results they found after showing children cartoons point, indeed, to the fact that media exposure had effects but also that these can only be seen in the short term and cannot be measured for the longer term. Such effects apparently dissipate quickly and are more a form of excitement.

Another kind of research that psychologists do is survey research. This is quantitative research that relies on a set of techniques based on aselect data collection and statistical data analysis. These allow a researcher to say something about larger groups of individuals. Patti Valkenburg found that most teenagers are not greatly influenced in a negative way by their social media use and enjoy benefits. A small group, however, feels bad about themselves after extended social media use. She is careful to emphasize that we should not demonize social media but do need to be aware of the risk they pose for a vulnerable group (see Valkenburg, Meyer and Beyens 2022).

Qualitative audience researchers are not averse to understanding vulnerability but they know they do not have the tools to say something about individual persons (we are not therapists or psychoanalysts) nor about 'populations' (large groups of individuals). We feel it is more useful to unravel the different layers of meaning-making that are involved in for instance gaming. We might focus on affordances, feelings, the assumption of filter bubbles or the friendships gamers talk about. We look at their world through their eyes rather than at them and, thus, develop a different kind of knowledge of how media matter.

Another term that is used in qualitative audience research at the level of the individual is **identity**. This too is an important one as it speaks to our sense of self in relation to others. Identity is not personality or a person's core self says Kathryn Woodward (2004, 13). Rather, identity is the interface between (a) a social role, (b) the way a person performs that role, (c) the emotions and feelings they have and (d) how others perceive them being that particular person. Identity always depends on difference (what you are not) and on community (being the same as some and different from others). Identity has to do with performance as the sociologist Erving Goffman defined it (1990). Woodward adds that if identity is the 'interface between the personal and the social, we need to take the social, cultural and economic factors into account which shape experience. How are we able to take up some identities and not others' (Woodward 2004, 18)? The extent to which we have agency or are at the mercy of others can differ significantly. Identity, therefore, requires understanding of how power, ideology and the myths people believe in are relevant.

Second level: media practices and/as meaning-making

Via identity, we can connect (everyday) meaning-making, which is what audience research wants to know about, with understanding how societies function. Stuart Hall called that link 'the cultural circuit'. He said that meaning is what gives us a sense of our own identity, of who we are and with whom we 'belong'. The circuit moves from meaning-making to culture and how it helps us mark out and maintain identity within groups and the differences between them (1997, 3). Meaning-making and identity formation are deeply connected. Culture is the space where they meet.

Stepping away from the level of individuality, personhood and subjectivity, we come to the crossroads where media matter. This is the intersection between culture, identity and belonging. Put differently: human beings rely on storytelling to understand the world. Storytelling is what the media provide us with. We need to know what dangers to avoid, we like to feel safe and warm and happy and from time to time we like excitement and sensation. In oral culture storytelling connected smaller groups of people. From hieroglyphs and other early scripts, we see how important it was felt to be to make sure that stories survive. Print media, cinema, radio and television take us in seven-mile boots to today's social media and cross-media culture which perform those very same functions.

Media do more than inform us about the world. They are also a kind of mirror that tells us about norms and codes and ideals. Both processes are referred to as 'representation'. As it is impossible to recreate the entire world, the media choose and select what to focus on and how. Simply making what is happening elsewhere present (or present again) is, therefore, a more complicated thing than it would seem. To clarify, representation can be read as what members of parliament do. They make the people present who have voted for them (or they should in any case). They are stand-ins. It is also what a photo or a video or a newspaper article does. It stands in for what happened somewhere, whether in the real world or on a stage or in a studio. Such standing-in produces something new though. Stuart Hall distinguished between three different ways to understand representation. We can think of representation as simply *reflection*. Then, it is always about words or video technique imitating the true meaning of an event or a person. Or we can bring in *intention*: what did the writer or director want us to think when reading or watching this? Hall himself preferred thinking of representation in terms of *construction*. In making sense of reality, we decipher relevant languages. We recognize how signs connect objects and meaning through codes and conventions. Hall points out that this means that representation does not happen after an original event: representation itself is constitutive of the event (see Hall 1997, 16–64).

As media researchers, we know that media-created realities may appear lifelike and 'natural' but they are *new* images. Depending on what lens or filters have been used, what words are spoken or added as a tag, what is focused on and what is left out, we may interpret that new image very differently. Given that in representation something new comes into being, it will matter to people how they are represented: the media regularly get it wrong. Early feminist media critique spoke of 'symbolic annihilation' (Tuchman 1978). We still see far less women than men when we watch the news for instance. The media can be deeply invested in stereotypes that are a burden for those represented. Think of how women who wear a hijab are represented as victims. That lessens your chances to get a job as you are not seen as an independent woman who can make up her own mind.

Representation is closely related to **stereotypes**. In itself it is not a problem that we rely on shortcuts to ideas about (groups of) other people. It makes social interaction easier. When stereotypes become 'truth' though, there is a problem because stereotypes then flatten and reduce social reality and how it came into being. Notably, unequal power relations are lost. When you do audience research, it is important to check in with interviewees about how they 'identify'. That way you make sure you respect the other person's wishes and feelings. It helps you gain access to their world and meaning-making. When they themselves use stereotypes, you always need to ask follow-up questions to find out whether and with what kind of truths the stereotypes used are associated.

Ultimately, stereotypes are lodged in ideologies, or world views. As ideology denotes a comprehensive picture of how societies function, 'discourse' is often used as a slightly more manageable term. **Discourse** can simply mean talk. In the constructivist tradition that we are working in, discourse is taken to mean: everything that can and cannot be said about a particular subject within a specific context and a specific period. That may not sound that much smaller than 'ideology' but it is. A discourse can pertain to sexuality, to labor, to marriage. Where discourses overlap, interesting things happen, both in speech and in how we interpret social practices. For some, talking about sexuality will be a discussion of work. For others, it might be about marriage and, therefore, about property rights; for others, still it might be about love or about lust or about secrecy. For a constructivist, these large language networks are always connected with social practices. That means that discourse does not only change because language changes over time but also because power relations in social practices work in such a way that rules and norms over how to understand the world or do things will be under pressure. To continue with the meanings of the word 'sex:' today they are vastly different from what sex was taken to be halfway through the twentieth century. We have moved from procreation and illicit pleasure, to freedom and emancipation, to self-expression and consent. Who knows what it will refer to in another 70 years given artificial intelligence and augmented reality developments.

Talking about meaning and meaning-making is about more than definitions, rules or norms. Feelings come into meaning-making as well. Feelings require coming into some form of body or spoken language. The moment feelings are 'performed', they are called emotions. **Affect** is a term often used to denote the engine behind the performance of feelings. Although a tricky term, it is useful to try and understand it as it points to how in interrelating with the world and with others, there is energy that we feel. Whether for good or bad, energy is generated all the time (Wetherell 2012). Sara Ahmed (2004) uses the term 'affective economies' to describe how emotions (or socially performed feelings) bind people together into collectivities, taking on a life of their own. In Ahmed's work, the example is Aryan Nation, a supremacist ultra-right wing group whose hatred of anyone not racially 'white' connects them. Remember how, above, we point to the difference between what people say and what they do. When speaking of affect, the same type of distinction holds: affect is what moves people, not what they are. The difference may be minimal, but for an audience researcher, it is important, e.g., not to assume that all avid viewers of a television show are fans. Fans, in this type of research, are those who define themselves as such.

A last concept in this second set is **cultural citizenship**. It refers to belonging. The citizenship part is about the rights and responsibilities that we have. 'Cultural' refers to a specific kind of citizenship. In the 1980s, Renato Rosaldo wrote that cultural citizenship is "the right to difference" (1986). This is exactly what makes it an important concept: we use culture, including television or gaming, to learn about our rights and responsibilities, we exert and discuss them. For audience researchers, cultural citizenship refers to ongoing dialogue. It is spontaneous cultural and political critique that makes clear how emotion, affect and reasoning are deeply intertwined. Such critique often remains implicit. It needs us as researchers to understand how discipline and freedom unfold in the domain of culture as Toby Miller (2007) has put it. In Chapter 9, we use the concept to disentangle discussion of gender.

Third level: methodology

Television, social media, games, newspapers offer more than simple uses and gratifications, even if those are part of media use. They are entangled with processes of meaning-making and social power relations and themselves platforms of meaning-making that audiences reflect upon in an ultimately circular logic. What we need, therefore, are tools that allow us to approach audiences and media texts and practices with an open mind. Such tools are called **methods**. A set of interlinked methods and principles for using them is called a methodology. Methodologies link a particular philosophy or theory to an appropriate research method. They bridge philosophical notions and practical and applicable research strategies (Byrne 2001, 830).

This book's theory is that media are key sites of social meaning-making and, therefore, where culture is built and maintained. We also assume that media texts cannot *impose* how they are made meaningful (even if they can make powerful suggestions). We see individual subjects as 'nodal' points in the networks of meanings and material practices that make up a society. Although people use language as given, they will, in using it, either change or confirm established meanings, norms and identities. Given the wealth of media texts and talk, we consider it unlikely that researchers will be able to find single texts as having an identifiable effect either on people or on social and cultural practices. At the same time, we recognize that this is exactly what many people think the media can do. Ideologically, our society tends to accord much power to the media. Our methods of research, therefore, have to allow for open and respectful conversations in which it is possible for researchers and the researched to disagree.

Media ethnography and its open research methods allow exactly that kind of respectful exchange. Most of its key terms such as meaning and social practice are easy to understand. A second set of methodological terms define the relationship of the researcher to the kind of knowledge they produce. Hammersley and Atkinson (2019) speak of naturalism and constructivism. Often used in this regard are also objectivity, subjectivity and reflexivity. They refer to whether as a researcher we are looking for and expect to find predefined (objective) knowledge; that we can only give our very own definitions of what we see (subjective knowledge) or that we can move back and forth between different perspectives on the world and take into account that all perspectives on it will have been shaped by the circumstances in which they were built (reflexivity). Because we believe that meaning is constructed, rather than given, we set great store by reflexivity. That means asking questions such as: how did it matter for the interview or the participant observation fieldwork that I am a woman or nonbinary, present as queer or cis-gender, that I am short or tall, Asian, of color, white, older or younger? How is my reading of a particular media text shaped by the contexts of my everyday life, my privileges, ability or disability, my early-life experiences and upbringing? How might the reading of that particular text have been shaped by other texts?

Such reflection needs to take place before doing empirical research. It is called examining your 'preconceived notions'. They should not cloud your encounters with others. Researchers will often make a topic list with just a few key words to use in an interview which refer to the themes that are to be brought up in discussion. Such topic lists should not merely reflect your own ideas but allow for exploring what preconceptions and associative meanings they have for your informant. This is the reason that questionnaires are not often used in media ethnography. They tend to be built on closed questions and leave little room for the notions and ideas interviewees would like to bring to the conversation. They therefore give little insight into what ethnographers call 'members' categories': the terms and words used in a community that help to define the community's world.

Interviews are transcribed and are then called 'data'. Together with research memo's (the notes a researcher keeps in a diary, or a digital dated file), they are the basic research material that is then 'coded'. A code is simply a way of identifying with as little words as possible what is remarkable about a bit of interview. They are a way of summarizing what is said across different interviews when all the codes given are assembled and sorted into sets of similar meaning. As we are less interested in individuals than in collective meaning-making, we need analysis to bring out what is shared and what are idiosyncrasies (or the uniquely individual things that people say). Once the data (whether interview material or online discussions) are coded, open codes are 'clustered'. That is to say that they are brought together in groups to afford the researcher overview. This is an intuitive process. It usually takes several goes before a satisfactory list of open codes is drawn up and is clustered to satisfaction. Depending on the methodological approach used, these clusters are referred to as themes or as 'axial' codes.

The term axial code comes from **grounded theory**. Over the years, this mid-twentieth-century method of data analysis and generating theory has been shaped into a handy schematic for qualitative research. It organizes data reduction and analysis (going from the full transcripts to a list and then to clusters of codes) in three steps. The first two are *open* and *axial* coding. In axial coding, clusters are named that provide an overview focused on how meaning is made collectively across the group of interviewees or the data set used, which, e.g., consists of a Reddit discussion, or TV Time or YouTube comments. A careful check of the underlying quotes of the axial codes brings out whether the open codes worked well and the quotes share a way of referencing a particular phenomenon. The axial code 'television is dangerous' can refer back to quotes about limiting viewing time, to violent content or even to commercialism and commodification. In a larger research project, there will be a significant number of axial codes which then are further reduced by grouping them into 'selective' codes. The selective codes are the first step in the storytelling that the research article, report or thesis will do.

Research example: a coding tree in practice

Not so difficult to guess perhaps what this research project was about? At the same time, without quotes from the original material, which were interview transcripts conducted by Sarieke Hoeksma for her MA thesis, it can be hard to follow the logic of coding tree.

Open Coding	Axial Coding	Selective Coding
boys	nature versus nurture	'Be who you are'
typically boys	to be yourself	'Big, bad world'
typical boys	to be protected	'Do not hold me
girls	risk zone	accountable'
typically girls	gender experiments are	
typically girl	a phase	
aggression	Television is dangerous	
pink		
tough		
what children prefer		
good television viewing		
habits		
bad television viewing		
habits		
nostalgia		
commercialization		

These are codes given in interviews with parents. The project was meant to identify ways in which gender conventions could become less dichotomous in children's television. Instead of being enlisted for change, as Hoeksma had expected, the parents offered three completely different interpretative repertoires to talk about raising children and the role of television. Selective coding showed they managed to combine deeply liberal convictions (Be who you are), with great fear of bullying and how unforgiving society is to individuals who present as 'different' (big, bad world) and feeling that parents have a tough job: children will do their own thing (Do not hold me accountable). Needless to say, they saw television as a potential risk and certainly were not advocates of television putting ideas in their children's heads (see Hermes and Hoeksma 2024).

Selective codes can deliver themes (at a higher level of abstraction than axial codes do) but also 'repertoires', 'discourses', 'vocabularies' or 'frames'. Which of these terms is used is really a matter of personal preference of a researcher. When using *repertoire*, the reconstruction of the structure of meaning-making around a certain subject or related to a set of media texts or practices is tied to recurring patterns of speech (Wetherell and Potter 1988). *Discourse* tends to refer to combinations of talk and material, social practices. *Vocabulary* can be preferred when groups or contexts are compared. It denotes appropriate ways of expressing oneself. *Frames* was introduced by Goffman. It makes clear how when some things are focused on and are taken into account, others stay outside of the frame and are declared to not be relevant or of interest. It gives a good sense of the constructedness of social meaning-making.

Interviewee, respondent, participant?

Viewers, listeners, users, fans, commenters, haters or dislikers – audience members have many names. Once they become part of a research project, there are even more: in ethnography, they are called informants. In a design project, they are either participants or (end) users. And in qualitative research project, they will usually be called an interviewee or a participant. In quantitative research, individuals disappear, and they are subsumed under the number of questionnaires that were completed (n = ...) and called respondents. Throughout this book, we mostly use 'interviewee' and 'participant' to highlight the agency and participation of, well, our participants in practices of meaning-making.

In visual and textual analysis and in sensory ethnography, additional concepts will come to the fore. As these are not key terms for qualitative audience research generally, they will not be focused on here. What is important to know is that we like qualitative audience research for how it allows us to combine the interpretation of texts and images with the ways in which they are made meaning of. We have no ultimate preference for the order in which these different parts of a project are undertaken. When a researcher has practiced working self-reflexively and is aware of her preconceived notions, she will not let the outcome of visual analysis or autoethnography (in which the researcher becomes her own research subject) blind her to what audiences say. If you are feeling you might still have a way to go in learning how to do this, we highly recommend *audience-led* forms of textual and visual analysis so that the voice of others is given proper attention.

References

Ahmed, Sara. 2004. "Affective Economies." *Social Text* 22 (2): 117–39. https://doi.org/10.1215/01642472-22-2_79-117.

Barthes, Roland. 1972. *Mythologies*. New York: Farrar, Straus and Giroux.

Bourdieu, Pierre. 1984. *Distinction: A Social Critique of the Judgement of Taste.* Cambridge, MA: Harvard Univ. Press.

Byrne, Michelle. 2001. "Grounded Theory as a Qualitative Research Methodology." *AORN Journal* 73 (6): 1155–56. https://doi.org/10.1016/S0001-2092(06)61841-3.

Goffman, Erving. 1990. *The Presentation of Self in Everyday Life*. 1. Anchor Books ed., rev. Ed. New York: Anchor Books.

Hall, Stuart. 1997. "The Work of Representation." In *Representation: Cultural Representations and Signifying Practices*, 16–64. Culture, Media, and Identities. London: Sage.

Hammersley, Martyn, and Paul Atkinson. 2019. *Ethnography: Principles in Practice*. 4th ed. New York: Routledge.

Hermes, Joke, and Sarieke Hoeksma. 2024. "Innocence." In *Cultural Citizenship and Popular Culture: The Art of Listening*. London/New York: Routledge.

Hill, Annette. 2019. *Media Experiences: Engaging with Drama and Reality Television*. London/New York: Routledge.

Miller, Toby. 2007. "Culture, Dislocation, and Citizenship." In *Global Migration, Social Change, and Cultural Transformation*, edited by Emory Elliott, Jasmine Payne, and Patricia Ploesch, 165–86. New York: Palgrave MacMillan.

Potter, John, and Margaret Wetherell. 1988. "Discourse Analysis and the Identification of Interpretative Repertoires." In *Analysing Everyday Explanation: A Casebook of Methods*, 168–83. London: Sage Publications.

Rosaldo, Renato, 1994, "Cultural Citizenship and Educational Democracy." *Cultural Anthropology*, 9 (3): 402–411.

Tuchman, Gaye. 1978. *Making News: A Study in the Construction of Reality*. New York: Free Press.

Valkenburg, Patti M., Adrian Meier, and Ine Beyens. 2022. "Social Media Use and Its Impact on Adolescent Mental Health: An Umbrella Review of the Evidence." *Current Opinion in Psychology* 44 (April): 58–68. https://doi.org/10.1016/j.copsyc.2021.08.017.

Wetherell, Margaret, and Jonathan Potter. 1988. "Discourse Analysis and the Identification of Interpretative Repertoires." In *Analysing Everyday Explanation. A Case Book*, 168–83. London: Sage.

Woodward, Kath, ed. 2004. *Questioning Identity: Gender, Class, Ethnicity*. 2nd ed. An Introduction to the Social Sciences Understanding Social Change. London/New York: Routledge.

Part II
Methods with method
A methodic overview
of engaging with audiences

3   Audience research
Methods of data collection and data analysis need one another ♥

Before introducing different methods of data collection and data analysis in the following chapters, this chapter focuses on the connection between the two. In research publications, you can often find brief summaries of how data were gathered – through surveys, interviews or life histories. Methods of textual analysis are also regularly introduced: semiotic analysis, narrative analysis, ideological critique. But how transcripts, online discussions or other audience materials are analyzed remains, far too often, a 'black box'. Without insight into how they were collected, data are meaningless. Any analysis of a haphazardly collected set of data is built on quicksand. That makes an accessible account of data collection important. Without knowing how good data were analyzed, even the most fascinating data become ... mere anecdote.

Data collection and data analysis need one another!

Neither data gathering nor data analysis is easy to do. Making things even more complicated, data come in very different shapes and forms. We need to have a sense of what we are looking for before we start collecting them. An obvious example is the difference between quantifiable answers – scores given in surveys, for instance, – and qualitative material – such as spontaneous conversation recorded during a participant design research project. Quantifiable answers do not give insight into what anthropologists call 'members' categories, should you be interested in those. Spontaneous conversation does provide such insight but does not allow for answering questions about groups of people beyond those present. Starting on a project, you need to also know how you want to analyze your data. Not every type of data collection fits with every type of data analysis. For the audience research introduced in this book, statistics and numbers are not very helpful. Our questions pertain to culture, meanings and feelings after all. While we will try to refrain from making jokes about 'dating' here, the underlying logic is the same: your data collection and data analysis need to match if you want the (intellectual) sparks to fly.

DOI: 10.4324/9781003315421-6

In the social and natural sciences, one of the recurring criteria for good research is whether or not the data collected and analyzed are 'representative'. In a political science survey, this might mean that you need to collect answers from a high number of people at different points in time before you can convincingly say something about shifting trends in voting. In a biochemical experiment, this might mean that you need to repeat the exact same process multiple times to confirm that the chemical reaction remains the same. In media and cultural studies, such forms of representativity are less important – but the ground rules of good research still apply. In practice, this means that all decisions made in the process of your research need to be accounted for explicitly and reflected on. From this understanding of research as a series of choices, this chapter functions as an introduction into the *empirical cycle of audience research* from initial idea, to saturation in data gathering (found in a process of continuous analysis), to theorization. In larger research projects, this cycle will be iterated – repeated – several times (Figure 3.1).

The outcomes of an iteration of the cycle will lead to new questions that need new data. The new data will need analyzing and theorizing. Theorization may again lead to new questions, and a third cycle starts. Developing theory might sound scary. Actually, it is no more (or less) than assessing what your material is telling you in relation to the questions you want answered. What kind of story are you finding yourself in?

Decisions, decisions, decisions: finding the right method for your project

The 'right' method is often chosen on the basis of what you have read about or already have some experience with. You may well think that analyzing television viewing needs to be based on viewer statistics or survey research that uses questionnaires. True enough, television audience research methods *can* be (and often are) quantitative: when you search for different methods of doing audience research, many of the easily accessible examples will come from the social sciences and from social psychology. For small-scale projects, these work less well. Good quantitative research needs to follow a somewhat different logic than the qualitative research discussed in this book. Quantitative research starts by developing hypotheses and then proceeds by 'testing' these. Hypotheses are formulated as true-false dichotomies. For a cultural studies – or humanities researcher – this can be a bit limiting. Grayscales fit us better! Instead of looking to the social sciences, our interest in cultural logics and cultural negotiations is better served by qualitative research approaches established in anthropology, sociology and cultural studies. They have the enormous advantage of working very well for small-scale student and early career projects. Of course, this also means that we are asking – and answering – different research questions with these qualitative methods.

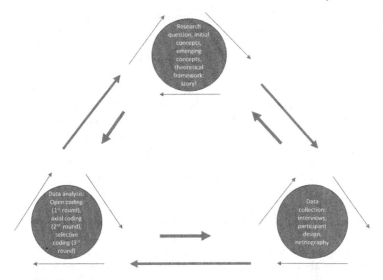

Figure 3.1 The Empirical Cycle. This is a very precise version of the empirical cycle for qualitative research, developed by Hutter and Hennink. It shows how the empirical cycle is actually a series of cyclical moments. Cyclical here means that you go round and round a couple of times before moving on. Cycles are not stages. Nor, as you can see, is there pressure to move in a particular direction or to start at a particular point. Sometimes an overheard anecdote is used to develop an initial set of codes. At other times, a project starts with a proper question or with an idea for a design research instrument. That might be a game or an activity such as drawing maps to address how the media landscape makes sense and what is to like and to be feared there. (For more on the empirical cycle see: Hutter, Hennink & Bailey 2020: 5).

So, it is not that one method is better than the other – just that some might be a better match. Even on the 'qualitative' side of things, there are different methods at your disposal, depending on what you want to know – which (research) question you are asking. They range from interviews, to diaries, to reconstructing biographies, to participant design or observation or using conversations that are published online on social media platforms.

In television audience research, we tend to have questions that have to do with representation and identity, with pleasure and power and with practices and rituals. All of these tell us something about meaning-making in everyday life. Some classic examples from the beginnings of television audience studies are David Morley's interviews in households in *Family Television*, Ann Gray's interviews with individual women about the video recorders in their homes in *Video Playtime* or Ien Ang's analysis of the letters people wrote to her about the prime-time soap opera *Dallas* (Ang 1985; Gray 1992; Morley 1986). The methods used by these researchers all have a link to what can broadly be termed media ethnography. Ethnography (derived from the Greek words for 'people' + 'writing') is a form of immersion. It gives us access to the experience of audiences with and through media. It can start by querying our own experiences as viewers (Ien Ang was a *Dallas* viewer herself who had had 'odd' reactions when people heard she watched the soap opera); by asking others about their experiences in interviews; by reading what they write online. We sometimes rely on the reports of other professionals who write about audiences. To explore how audiences 'make meaning', how they think about specific genres or specific televisual texts, about a cross-media phenomenon or an abstract concept, the ethnographic toolkit offers you a variety of starting points (more about this in *Chapter 4: Ethnography*). They will lead you to different forms of knowledge and to different stories. What's important in your choice of method for each project is exactly this: being aware that you are making a choice.

For a research project on 'casting and gender', we tried and tested different methods from the ethnography toolbox. (Collaborative) auto-ethnography helped us interrogate our own memories of cross-dressing characters in films like *Some Like It Hot* and *Mrs. Doubtfire*; 'netnography' allowed us to chart how other people talk-online about the recasting of male legacy roles like *Dr. Who* and *James Bond* with female actors and Media Discourse Analysis pointed us to how media professionals 'represent' audiences and their opinions about the casting of transgender characters with cisgender actors. Like all methods, these come with their own sets of advantages and disadvantages.

- *Autoethnography* uses the researcher's own experiences as a form of data – and has the methodological merit of bringing one close to *irritation and unease with media texts*. It also offers uncoerced access to memory. Talking about our memories of (not) watching 'gender-bending' comedies showed us how the times have changed and how our tolerance for gender intolerance has greatly lessened. Despite having fond memories of *Some like it hot*, we realized that we are not tempted to rewatch old gender-benders when we come across them as offered on an old-fashioned tv channel or in one of the new library platforms.

- Should you be interested in *controversy*, collaborative auto-ethnography will not easily help you find it. *'Netnography'* is a better choice in that case. As a form of online ethnography, it follows conversations in semi-public online space and traces how cultural codes and identities are negotiated within communities of viewers and fans. Be warned: as a researcher, you might not like what you find. Exploring online comments on the re-casting of *Doctor Who* and *James Bond* for us meant that we had to take outright sexism seriously. It can be a real challenge to be open to definitions, intuitions and experiences that are diametrically opposed to your own. It is imperative to do so – but an enormous challenge at the same time.

The following chapters will introduce these methods (among others) in more detail, but you can see from this very short summary that methodological decisions matter. They allowed us to ask different questions and find different forms of answers: with collaborative autoethnography, we could explore our own viewing histories and memories, and how these informed our perception of casting decisions today. With netnography, we were able to trace how the casting of transgender characters with cisgender actors resonated differently for different communities of viewers. You see: different questions, different methods, different answers. Carefully testing and comparing the 'performances' of different methods reflects an ethic of care often applied to research subjects in scholarship but rarely to methodology itself. Thinking about what different forms of data collection and data analysis allow you (not) to do is the first step toward self-reflexivity (Figure 3.2).

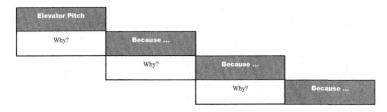

Figure 3.2 Peer Exercise: "Why, Why, Why". This exercise works well at the start of a research project: Person A gives a 30 second elevator pitch for *why* their primary media object should be researched (more) to Person B. After this pitch, Person B keeps on asking for more: why is this important, why this media object, why this platform, why this audience, why now, and so on – until Person A has fully convinced them. Try to make it to at least 3 answers, then switch roles. Taking notes of your answers (or asking Person C to do this for you) will help you when writing up your methodological decision-making.

Data collection: when is enough 'enough'?

In media and cultural studies, 'data' can come from all sorts of places. Television as a 'text' provides us with data to analyze, as do reviews and critiques in newspapers and online forums. Audiences themselves, of course, also provide you with data via observation or conversation, online or offline. The steps of data collection, then, are fairly straightforward:

1 *You identify interesting material (given your research topic).*
   This starting point for your research might come to you immediately, or there might be a phase of trial and error. Find out what is talked about where to narrow down options.
2 *You collect the data.*
   This is where it gets practical – you do interviews, focus groups, extract social media comments or trace online conversations.
3 *You keep notes of the decisions you make along the way.*
   These notes are sometimes also referred to as 'research memos.' They function both as a reminder for yourself about which decisions you made (about who to interview, for instance) and as a way to make your research process transparent. They can be quoted in your thesis or in a paper or article.

In the two research examples below, you can see two different approaches to data collection: for the case study on the Regency romance *Bridgerton*, a scraper tool was used to extract comments posted under a selection of YouTube videos. An archive of a specific moment in time was created. For our case study on the thriller/romance *You*, we collected and analyzed data in multiple rounds to ensure that the story we found was not just connected to one individual platform or moment in time but representative of a larger sociocultural phenomenon.

When has enough data been collected and how did different types of data and data collection inform our analysis? As you become more and more involved in the audience conversations you are tracing, you might realize that there is always *more* to look at. More interviews to be conducted, more threads to read, more reviews to check. And while this might sound counterintuitive: *A key part of data collection is knowing when to stop.* Qualitative research handbooks speak of reaching saturation. This simply means that after repeated tries (a new type of situation, example or informant), no new information or insights surfaced. Important: when making memos on how decisions were reached, record when and why you *stopped* data collection, why you moved on again and where to.

When you reach saturation, your research shifts from data collection to data analysis. Analysis initially is a simple process of data reduction.

It means deciding on what quotes, tropes or examples are meaningful and which are not. As described in Chapter 2, grounded theory's procedure of coding in three distinct phases is a useful way of doing this. Below some other options are listed.

Practice example *Bridgerton:* We burn for … Data Collection!

1 We began to look for online reactions to the tv series *Bridgerton* by simply searching for the show on Google – and noticed that 'reaction videos' on YouTube were among the top results.

2 We moved our search to YouTube and used the keywords 'Bridgerton' and 'reaction' to get an overview of the number, length and popularity of reaction videos.

3 We identified a number of channels that recorded and published videos of their reactions to watching *Bridgerton*. The criteria that were used to select channels for analysis were guided primarily by YouTube's own metrics published with videos: quantified levels of engagement measured in numbers of subscribers to a channel and views of a video, along with the number of comments that were left below the videos within the YouTube interface.

4 We found, rather unexpectedly, that the videos that elicited the most engagement are made by men and that, for the most part, the most popular reaction videos feature two or more (young) men offering commentary. In comparison, we noticed that women's reaction videos had less views on the individual videos and less subscribers on their channels.

5 We watched quite a few of these reaction videos and got the impression that women reacting mainly sought to criticize and educate – both regarding romance and race – and they mainly came to *Bridgerton* from familiarity with the romance genre. The men recording their reaction, however, were filled with wonder. They did not understand the conventions. This made for funny videos and interesting comments. It also opened up a search for 'cultural citizenship'.

6 We zoomed in on reactions to five different channels – following the crowd, we decided to analyze the comments under the videos with the highest numbers of viewers and subscribers and found ourselves watching men watching *Bridgerton*.

7 We used a so-called scraper tool, an automated data extraction tool developed by Bernard Rieder, to collect the

comments posted underneath these videos. Automation saved us endless clicking and copy/pasting. You can find a number of free tools for online data collection here: https://github.com/bernorieder.
8 We surveyed the comments to make sure that the data were both productive and fitted the scope and timeframe of this project – two other important considerations to take into account for your own data collection.

If you want to know what we did with these data, read about it in *Chapter 9: Data Analysis in Practice.*

Data analysis: finding your theme

Once you have your data collected, you will want to do more than marvel. But ... what *can* you do with data? The obvious answer: you analyze them!

1 *You can count.*
  This involves deciding what you count – and whether high or low numbers are especially meaningful. Try to challenge yourself to also see what's not there, what's missing.
2 *You can summarize.*
  This means describing what you notice in the data in your own words. This has the risk of simply repeating your research questions (and 'automatically' confirming your own hypotheses).
3 *You can compare.*
  This means using your data as a point of comparison – to other case studies or to the available literature. As with all decisions in your research process, you will need a justification for choosing this point of comparison.
4 *You can code.*
  Through 'coding' – not the hacker way, but the qualitative way – you take your data apart into small parts, fragments of sentences, codes and keywords, to shuffle them in order to reveal the 'bigger picture'.
5 *You can cluster your codes.*
  When you cluster your data, you first code to then notice emerging patterns related to theories or concepts or trends. Check with the available literature whether you are not missing something

6 *You can tilt perspectives.*
    In the coding process described further below, this tilting of perspectives is called 'selective coding' – and basically means that you are zooming out to get at the bigger picture
7 *You can collaborate.*
    When working on larger projects, you might have more than one person coding. How do you make sure that you are 'noticing' the same things? (This is called 'intercoder reliability' in quantitative research). In qualitative research you compare how you code until it feels right.
8 *You can do all of the above.*

The greatest challenge in data analysis is to allow the data you have collected to tell their own story. The first three forms are descriptive and deductive – which has its merits. We hope you are inspired to take up one of the later forms of data analysis. In academic terms, they are referred to as 'inductive' research: rather than testing existing theory in a dataset, inductive research aims at *developing* theory. While we acknowledge that this might sound scary, we believe this is a doable challenge. Being open to finding unexpected themes in your data, ones you have not searched for, is the first step toward theorization. Instead of imposing preexisting ideas onto what informants say, this methodological mindset means that you allow your data to guide you through your analysis – toward new stories.

Theorizing is storytelling

Theorizing is actually something most of us do on a daily basis. It is to think about what we observe, develop possible explanations and relate these to concepts. Concepts are abstract summaries of how we understand and deal with physical or virtual reality, with fantasy, with feelings and emotions, with who we are. You can also think of it as modeling (what relates to what, and how?). Even better is thinking of it as storytelling. In storytelling, concepts can behave like characters: some are real heroes, others are supporting characters and some, actually, villains. In audience studies, a number of concepts tend to return. Earlier representation, identity, power and everyday life are mentioned as some of the concepts that frame this particular field. Theorizing is basically combining two or more of these concepts and expanding on them: how do audiences make meaning or 'sense' of a television show like *You* while navigating the boundary between reality and fantasy? How does previous knowledge of Regency romance novels change viewer response to depictions of nonconsensual sex?

In both of these case studies, television becomes a lens to explore larger questions of contemporary life. Deciding which methods of data collection and analysis to use, changes the story you can tell (convincingly) about how audiences negotiate answers to these questions. Evocative labels are a good way to theorize. The moment we systematize the outcome of our testing, or, in qualitative inquiry, reflect on our labels, we come to a new type of story about the world. These are not stories based on our imagination alone, they are based on systematic observation and checking those observations and the ideas we developed on the basis of it, to the available literature.

Coding on paper vs. in spreadsheets vs. with software

When it comes to coding, there are no strict 'rules' on how to do this best. One of us prefers to print interview transcripts and code them with a variety of highlighters, the other prefers spreadsheets. While coding on paper might make it easier to notice important parts (and provide a welcome screen break for your eyes), using spreadsheets like Excel or Google Sheets comes with search and select functions (and an 'undo' button). In addition to these manual forms of coding, there is also a variety of qualitative data analysis software, for instance MaxQDA, N-Vivo or Atlas-ti, that are especially good at visualizing your coding. Give it a try and find out what works best for you!

Research example *You*: "well, hello there. Who are you?"

Our case study of the Netflix series *You* – following Penn Badgley as a 'lovable' (with a strong question mark) stalker extraordinaire in his pursuit of increasingly complicated relationships – emphasizes how data collection and data analysis are not steps that follow one after the other, but rather go hand in hand in finding a story.

Data collection – Round 1

We first had the idea to explore how *You* is negotiated in the semi-public sphere of online communities through the humorous-but-critical responses of the series' star Penn Badgley on tweets romanticizing his character. As discussed in the previous section on 'Data Collection', this was the first decision with consequences for the story we could tell. Next, we extracted tweets posted around the release date of the second season on Netflix using an open-source archiving tool. To make the dataset productive for the project we had in mind, we limited our data collection to tweets in English (but posted from anywhere) and using a predefined set of hashtags. Including the hashtag #You did not work well for our data collection as it yielded more tweets than we could handle.

Open coding – Round 1

In open coding, this meant highlighting the words and sentences that stood out. As tweets (at least at the time) were limited to 140 characters the open coding occasionally also meant highlighting the entire tweet – although we tried to avoid this to keep our highlights manageable. Some like using different colors even in open coding. See what works for you. A best practice tip: try to read through your data multiple times – taking more and more time as you do so. Don't overthink what could or could not be important, but let your data speak for itself.

So how can I be rooting for a **murderous psychopath that's just a nice guy** 😔. **Mind messed up!**
#YouNetflix

#You #YouNetflix Trying to decide if Joe was all bad after binge watching the 1st season:

I really enjoyed #YouNetflix. **But it makes me feel bad that end up rooting for an unrepentant murderer/stalker.**

#YouNetflix I should be against this guy that kills for love , but here I am feeling like I understand. **Lol I don't like things that confuse my integrity**
😂😂😂💀🎃

Okay, Joe Goldberg is hot. I think I have some issues. #YOUNetflix #JoeGoldberg #whatswrongwithme

---

if love's baby turns out to be milo's and not joe's then it's gonna be another gossip girl situation **#gossipgirl #YouNetflix #YOUSEASON2**

Data collection – Round 2

Open coding gave us a first sense, a first 'feel', of the data. As we were interested in larger questions of how viewers navigate their (conflicting) responses to the series, we decided that we wanted to include more than one platform. As the timeframe of our research coincided with the release (and promotion) of the second series, we included the comments posted underneath the respective trailers of the first and second season on YouTube. Considering the different organizational logics and levels of anonymity of Twitter and YouTube, the inclusion of YouTube comments allowed for a provisional testing of the themes developed through the coding of comments posted on Twitter. Understanding meaning-making processes as not just platform-specific, but representative of a broader cultural phenomenon, is strengthened by combining the two data sources.

Open coding – Round 2

Combining the YouTube comments with the extracted tweets, we did another round of open coding. We grouped the open codes together under 'speaking' labels. While in open coding you might highlight sentences or even entire passages (especially when using interviews or longer statements), actual labels should be shorter. For our case study, these labels

So how can I be rooting for a murderous psychopath that's just a nice guy 😕. Mind messed up! #YouNetflix	'Is this normal?'
#You #YouNetflix Trying to decide if Joe was all bad after binge watching the 1st season:	
I really enjoyed #YouNetflix. But it makes me feel bad that end up rooting for an unrepentant murderer/stalker.	Self-reflection
#YouNetflix I should be against this guy that kills for love , but here I am feeling like I understand. Lol I don't like things that confuse my integrity 😩😩😩😕🥴	Self-reflection, 'Is this normal?'
Okay, Joe Goldberg is hot. I think I have some issues. #YOUNetflix #JoeGoldberg #whatswrongwithme	
if love's baby turns out to be milo's and not joe's then it's gonna be another gossip girl situation #gossipgirl #YouNetflix #YOUSEASON2	Reference to *Gossip Girl*

included, among others: *looking for approval, moral judgment of the character and his actions, 'is this normal?', personal experiences, self-reflexion, physical descriptions, references to the actor* and *references to other series.* If you do this coding in a spreadsheet, you can place these labels in the column next to your quotes. As you are aiming to 'find' the story within your data, it is fully okay if you don't have anything to highlight or label for some of your data and if some quotes fit with multiple labels.

Axial coding

Open Coding	Axial Coding
Looking for approval · "Is this normal?" · Community (we) · Ambivalence	*Validation*
Realism judgements · References to other series · Personal experiences	*Knowledge*
Conditionality (if/would) · Individuality (I) · Romantic hero Ideal masculinity	*Fantasy*
Explanations · Emphasis on (good) intentions · "Anything for love"	*Idealization*
Physical descriptions · Attractiveness/Sexyness · "What is beautiful is good"	*Appearance*
References to the actor · Comparison to other roles · Deflection	*Resemblance*

In a second round of axial coding, these labels were connected and grouped into six themes: *validation, knowledge, fantasy, idealization, appearance* and *resemblance*. In this form of coding, you try to find broad connections between the labels you have come up with in open coding. Moving from the 'note' style of your open codes, your axial codes should be concrete keywords – and could already point to specific concepts or overarching themes.

Selective coding

Through selective coding, we narrowed down three interpretative repertoires – *Experience, Fantasy* and *Embodiment* – which represent different strategies viewers employ to understand and explain their love for the series and its questionable main protagonist. To tell the story of your research, you trace these interpretative repertoires back to the original comments or quotes – some of which will be included in your paper or publication to validate your conclusions. In a way, you are moving back to your 'raw data' here – which also shows why recording the individual steps of your coding process is crucial.

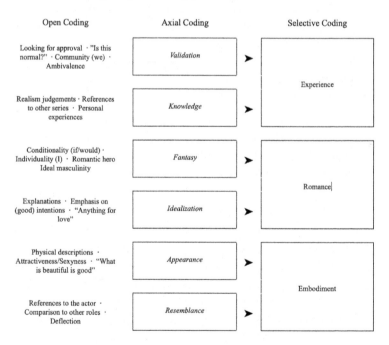

You can read more about *You* in Chapter 8: *Discourse Analysis in Practice.*

**Exercise: template for your own
coding tree (in 3 Steps)**

The coding tree is a way to visualize your storytelling – and trace the connections between your codes as you 'build' towards your repertoires. You can find two different templates to structure your data from open to axial and selective coding.

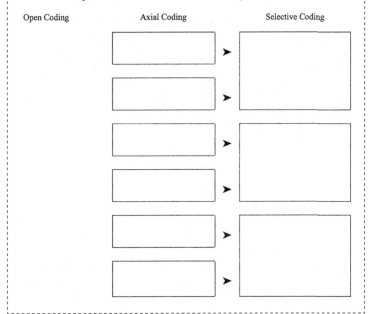

References

Ang, Ien. 1985. *Watching Dallas: Soap Opera and the Melodramatic Imagination.* London: Routledge.

Gray, Ann. 1992. *Video Playtime: The Gendering of a Leisure Technology.* Comedia. London/New York: Routledge.

Morley, David. 1986. *Family Television: Cultural Power and Domestic Leisure.* Comedia Series, no. 37. London: Comedia Pub. Group.

4 Ethnography

Or: how to understand the value of presence

WITH MARIAM YASSEIN

Anthropologists and ethnographers are accustomed to reflecting on their own 'presence' in a field: would the interactions they witness have happened anyway? Would the story they are being told have been the same if they looked different or presented themselves differently? *How data is collected matters.* While the field of audience research might be a bit different, there is much we can learn from how anthropologists developed ethnography.

In qualitative audience research, the researcher is always present

What exactly 'ethnography' entails can be difficult to grasp. Ethnography as a field has changed profoundly over the last decades and continues to change. From being mostly interested in describing 'other' cultures, the attention of contemporary ethnography has shifted to "settings nearer to home" (Draper 2015, 36). What has remained the same, however, is that ethnography directly relates to people – and their practices. As media researchers, we tend to rely less on extended participant observation and long sojourns in 'the field', but we know ourselves informed by ethnography and indebted to 'the ethnographic turn' in cultural studies (Drotner 1994; Schrøder 1994). This chapter explores how the principles of ethnography can be adapted and applied to media studies – and how to balance our own experience with those of others in an ethical and caring way. Moving across personal and anonymous, 'real' and 'virtual', popular and professional discussions, we highlight how being present and paying attention to practices is the basis for reflexivity and crucial for good audience research.

Instead of contextualizing the complex field of ethnography, this chapter suggests understanding ethnography as a **'toolbox'**. Some of its tools may be a bit rusty (but still fairly functional), and some are

DOI: 10.4324/9781003315421-7

new additions (but need to be tried out first). What's important in the dictionary definition of 'tool' is that it's something that helps you do or achieve something. That is exactly what methods are, too! The 'toolbox' analogy underlines an important aspect of research. Not every tool works for every task. The DIYers among you might have tried to use the back of a screwdriver as a hammer. Kind of works but your thumbs and the wall would have preferred a hammer. The 'toolbox' also helps us understand doing audience research as a practice – something you can learn, and something you get better at the more you do it. Also, as our screwdriver example emphasizes, finding creative solutions and alternative approaches is half the fun. Even if it is a bit painful at first...

Ethnography and ethics: something to think about

Thinking about ethics *before* you start your research and *while* you are conducting your research is a crucial practice of care. An obvious example: doing interviews with young children, for instance, always requires the consent of their parents beforehand. This requires you to be aware of the types of questions you can ask, and how long you will try to make children sit through an interview. What you need to think about as it comes to ethics depends on your topic, your participants and the method you choose.

With observations, you need to be aware of who you are observing where and what people are doing. These situations might change or play out differently because of your bodily presence. Think about observing a group of teenagers gathered around someone's smartphone in a skatepark, selecting, playing and watching short videos together. As a researcher who is also young and cool and nonthreatening, you will likely have ample time to watch the negotiation of 'what to watch next' unfold. As a researcher who is notably older, and does not easily blend in with the environment, you will probably seem like an intruder – and the group will move away quickly. As a 'neutral' observer, you might have a duty of care to intervene in situations that are potentially harmful.

Beyond blending in as an observer, a key ethical question is how you get access to the situations and communities you are observing or participating in. Especially if you are asking questions, the people you are observing need to know that you are a researcher – and that their answers are being recorded (either written down or recorded as audio/video/photography) and might be used in other contexts, outside of the setting they were made in. For interview projects, you, therefore, need the written consent of your interviewees to use and/or publish material afterward. Depending on the context and topic of your research, you should also guarantee that interviewees will be anonymized in your writing. For example, you can refer to your informant Claire as 'Respondent 1' for full anonymization or as 'Claudette' for a link to their gender and nationality as they have come to be established in the context of your research project.

There is another dimension to engaging with informants, both in online and offline spaces: safety. With this, we mean physical safety (thinking about where you meet interviewees), technological safety (thinking about which technologies you use to record and store data), but also emotional safety (thinking about what you are comfortable with, and what your participants are comfortable with). The last point, particularly, becomes more complex – and even more urgent – when you are exploring viewpoints that are very different from your own. For example, journalism researchers Karoline Andrea Ihlebæk and Carina Riborg Holter are interested in far-right politics. Such projects need extra special care of course which can involve how and where informants are interviewed:

> Because of the sensitivity of the topic, the informants were given the possibility to choose how they wanted to be interviewed. Though such variation in form was not ideal, the data still provides important in-depth insights into the worldview of a contested and largely unexplored group of media users.
>
> (Ihlebaek and Holter 2021, 1212)

Operating from a point of respect and care – for yourself and your interviewees – is paramount in all audience research.

'What happens online stays online?' While it might be easier to get access and blend in online communities than offline communities, the same ethical considerations apply. They involve identifying yourself as a researcher, especially when you are actively participating in conversations. For example, if you want to use an online forum like *Reddit* as a way to understand how audiences think about the depiction of Hijabi characters on the Spanish series *Élite*, you will have to decide whether you just want to read along a discussion as it unfolds, or whether you want to pose specific questions and follow up on previously made comments (as we do in Chapter 5). As technologies and platforms are changing, so are the ethical standards that apply to them. In early fan scholarship on online communities, it was quite common to publish user names with quotes in academic publications. The assumption was that user names were self-chosen and part of an online identity that does not necessarily link back to the real-life identity of the user. More recently, there has been a shift in this practice: for both closed communities, i.e., online spaces where you have to create an account and supply personal information to be able to see comments and conversations, and semi-closed communities, i.e., easily accessible spaces like *Reddit* or *X* (formerly *Twitter*), users are now considered to have a right to anonymity. In practice, this means that you either redact user names or change them.

The second option has the advantage of retaining some of the meaning attached to the user names as well. For example, a sexist comment about the casting of Jodi Whittaker as the 13th *Doctor Who* – a highly debated gender switch of a male legacy role – might read differently when connected to the username @MrMakeBritainGreatAgain than the user name @Snugglepuff (these are made-up names). When you change usernames, rather than use numbers or other impersonal labels, you can try to translate them doing as much justice as you can to the humor, the political or, e.g., regional distinctive elements you recognize in the original. As with all anonymization, you will need to keep track of which names you change to which pseudonyms – especially if you plan on returning to your data set at another time. In professional research projects, research data these days will be stored in specialized digital archives with a readme file.

Ethics, incorporated: the practical side of ethics

All of the ethical considerations discussed above have a bureaucratic side: project ideas might have to be officially approved, consent forms need to be signed and filed, data needs to be stored safely. Before you start doing ethnographic research, see whether there is an 'Ethics Board' at your university, and what their requirements and procedures look like. The specifics might vary slightly between different national contexts or even between different universities, but the principles are the same: the privacy of your respondents (and yours) needs to be protected. This continues after your research is completed – and could for instance require that you save your interview transcripts with password protection, or only on online databases with servers in Europe and under European privacy law. The more sensitive your collected data – because what your respondents say touches on politics, for instance, or because they shared sensitive and personal stories – the more you need to think about ethics as a practical issue as well. Confer with a supervisor or with colleagues when you think a form of aftercare is needed. Last but not least: if you hope to publish your work in an academic journal, know that many journals today require a copy of your university's ethics committee approval for your project.

Online/offline, here/there: ethnography in different environments

With terms like 'netnography', 'digital ethnography' or 'virtual ethnography', you might have already realized that ethnography increasingly pays attention to digital practices and digital interactions. Instead of thinking online and offline, old and new methods as dichotomies, we prefer to think of environments – and ask ourselves how different environments inform how we watch, experience and discuss television. How have our viewing practices at home changed with a second or even third screen nearby? Do online discussions of a beloved (or hated) show come up in offline conversations? Why there are still so many television sets in Portuguese restaurants – and how does that change the dynamics around the table? All of these questions are entangled with where, when and how we engage with different media objects. 'Environment', then, becomes both a question of the setting and the individual and social actions happening in, around and because of that setting.

Thinking about environments comes with questions of *access* and *authenticity*. You might not be able to get access to all settings and all respondents that you are interested in interviewing. Business executives for international cooperations like *Youku*, for example, are quite difficult to get a hold of. To make this easier, you could try out different ways to present yourself: calling yourself a student in a first email might open some doors and give you access to some respondents, while keeping you from others. The same goes for getting access to groups that you do or do not belong to: organizing a focus group with drag queens to discuss the latest season of *RuPaul's Drag Race* will be easier if you already have connections in the scene. But even if you don't: don't let that stop you! Sometimes, it just needs one participant to refer you to other people and vouch for you as a trustworthy researcher (something we call 'snowballing'). This links back to authenticity: keep true to yourself and don't pretend to be someone you are not. That is not just unethical (as discussed above) but also won't help your research in the long term.

Thinking about authenticity also applies to your participants, and the environments you observe or interview them in. An interview situation tends to be a bit awkward at first – especially if you are in the impersonal setting of a conference room at the university. Neither do online environments automatically reveal the 'authentic' selves of people. Tweeting a comment on a current news event is as (if not even more) constructed and performative as is answering an interview question. As a researcher, your main task is to reflect on these environments, and your position in them. Look beyond what you read, see and hear – to find deeper meanings. Hidden assumptions, hopes and fears come across in all sorts of interactions between people.

Getting to work: the 'ethnographic toolbox'

Ethnography as a field is deeply invested in the everyday practices of people. As an audience researcher, you can draw on the ethnographic toolbox to explore how different media are woven into these everyday practices. The availability of audience discussions on social media has been a boost to hearing, researching and discussing everyday talk and interpretation of media texts. Online discussions draw on and continue in offline settings as well, either with the same or with different people. In this sense, there is a bit of a looping logic at work here:

1 *The 'old' ethnographic methods help us to make sense of 'new' media.*
2 *These 'new' media might also help us to establish 'new' methods.*
3 *These 'new' methods allow us to analyze 'old' media differently than before.*

The methods featured in our 'ethnographic toolbox' are *observation, participant observation, netnography, auto-ethnography, collaborative auto-ethnography, the long interview, the focus group* and *media discourse analysis.* As with all methods, they come with their own advantages and challenges – summarize in Table 4.1. On the right-hand side, you will find suggestions for further reading.

Ethnographic Toolbox

A first overview of different ethnographic methods, their advantages and challenges, examples of these methods 'in action' and ideas for your own research:

Description	Advantages	Challenges	Examples
Method: **Observation**			
In ethnography, observation is a 'passive' form of participant observation: As a present outsider, you observe the practices of other individuals or groups, and take notes on what you observe.	Nothing is more 'everyday' than what is happening all around you– which is where your observation begins. Observing others in everyday situations might point you to questions that you had not considered before.	A lot of practices around television happen within the private sphere of the home – which you might not be able to access easily (please, no breaking and entering). However, with more and more 'mobile' viewing you could for instance observe media practices during your daily commute.	'Listening to a long conversation. An ethnographic approach to the study of information and communication technologies in the home' by Roger Silverstone, Eric Hirsch and David Morley in *Cultural Studies* (1991) James Lull (1988). *World families watch television.*
Method: **Participant Observation**			
In the best scenario, participant observation means hanging out with people, asking questions and taking notes. As the more active, more involved version of 'observation', participant observation means taking part in the activities of other people.	Participant observations allows you to experience something with and through your participants – and this experience, crucially, is more than just visually. How does it feel to be in a crowded bar surrounded by other fans of the *Eurovision Song Contest?* How are different technological devices handed around in the family home?	Participant observation can take a lot of time – for you to get into the 'feel' of different communities and situations, and for them to accept your presence in return. This is, of course, much easier when you do participant observation in communities that you already belong to – like a weekly viewing session with your friends, for instance, or a regular live screening of your favorite sports team competing.	*Television, Ethnicity and Cultural Change* by Marie Gillespie (1995) *Club cultures* by Sarah Thornton (1995)
Method: **(Family) Interviews in the Home**			
Whether done in a communal living room in a student house, in a nuclear family home or the sitting room of a nursing home, this form of group interview is close to participant observation but includes (long) interviews	How are different technological devices handed around in the family home?	See above.	*Family Television: Cultural Power and Domestic Leisure* by David Morley (1986)

Description	Advantages	Challenges	Examples
Method: Auto-Ethnography			
Auto-Ethnography turns the lens of ethnography onto the self: Observing and questioning your own life across its different contexts functions as a starting point to understand practices and perspectives that might be similar or different to the people around you.	In autoethnography, you draw a connection between the personal and the cultural. In other words: You are using your autobiography to do ethnographic research. With this shift, autoethnography does not focus on others – and does not assume a position of power as it comes to interpreting the practices of others.	With auto-ethnography, you need to be highly self-reflexive. In what ways can your individual experiences function as a ground for larger arguments about questions beyond your personal experience? Can you take enough distance from what shaped your life to understand larger patterns?	*Landscape for a Good Woman: A Story of Two Lives* by Carolyn Steedman (1982)
Method: Collaborative Autoethnography			
Collaborative autoethnography similarly uses the self – but in a collaborative format. In conversation with other researcher(s), you draw on your memories and experiences to see how your understanding of media objects and practices might be connected to larger settings.	The strengths of auto-ethnography plus the double advantage of having access to another and of being able to compare experiences. Through a repeating process of sharing, documenting and interpreting, collaborative autoethnography points you to patterns that might not be as visible as when doing this form of self-reflexive research by yourself.	Collaborative autoethnography requires not only self-reflexivity, but also a lot of trust in your collaborators – diving back into complex and complicated memories and experiences and talking about them without judging or feeling judged is not always easy.	*Collaborative Autoethnography* by Heewon Chang, Faith Ngunjiri and Kathy-Ann C Hernandez (2013)
Method: The Long Interview			
The long interview is – maybe – the most intensive method listed here as it comes to time and interaction. Interviewing people for a research project is different than interviewing for newspapers or magazines: you are not out to get specific information nor do you want to confirm your preconceptions. You want to be open to the unexpected in their stories.	Interviewing comes with the advantage of asking follow-up questions: You can ask your interviewee to explain or elaborate on something they said, and you can 'follow' your interviewers to topics and questions you might not have thought about before.	Not only does interviewing – and transcribing interviews – take time, but finding interviewees does as well. The more 'niche' your research topic is, the more tricky it might be to find enough people willing to be interviewed by you. Be aware that people cancel easily.	*Video Playtime The Gendering of a Leisure Technology* by Ann Gray (1992) *Dislike-Minded Media, Audiences, and the Dynamics of Taste* by Jonathan Gray (2021)

Description	Advantages	Challenges	Examples
Method: Focus Group			
Sometimes also called a 'group interview', the focus group brings together multiple people to discuss a certain topic. For audience research, this could also involve watching something together – a sports event, for instance, or the latest episode of a beloved series.	While the long interview focuses on one person at a time, the group interviews allows your respondents to expand on each other's answers – and you to ask whether something was felt or experienced by other interviewees in the same way.	All groups have specific dynamics – and knowing how to navigate these dynamics can be challenging, especially in the beginning of your research career. Plus, depending on the topics you are interested in, not every participant of your research group might be able and willing to speak up in front of the group about their own experiences.	Livingstone and Lunt (1991) *Talk on Television*, and Lunt and Livingstone (1996)
Method: Media Discourse Analysis			
Media Discourse Analysis is not always considered part of ethnography – you might also find this method listed under textual analysis, or discourse analysis. But: Media texts are both written by a specific audience (media professional) for a specific audience (depending on the publication) and often use and quote what these audiences have said elsewhere.	Media texts – newspaper and journal articles as well as audiovisual news – play an important role in informing the first-hand experience and meaning making that ethnography charts. How media professionals frame and interpret current issues and discussions works well as a starting point to chart an overview of public and publicized terms and positions. Especially because media impressions of debate, comments and critique become a reference point for audience members.	In media discourse, the complexity you might find in other discussions – both online and offline – is often lost. When audiences are presented as a collective in news media, individual differences are obliterated. Issues can needlessly be (further) politicized.	*The politics of hyperbole on Geordie Shore: Class, gender, youth and excess* by Helen Wood (2016)

This table is by no means exhaustive. There is also 'photo elicitation' – which means asking participants to take photos of something they notice and then interviewing them about these photos afterward. For Xanthe Glaw et al. (2017), a key advantage of this method is that it grants participants control of the topics talked about. There is 'archival ethnography' – which understands archives as a site for fieldwork. For Stephanie Decker and Alan McKinlay (2020), engaging with everyday practices as they are recorded in historical archives allows researchers to slow down and to spend more time checking and cross-referencing personal accounts. All of these methods have been used for research on everyday meaning-making as well. Should you have a great idea that you think might require yet a different method go for it! That's the great thing about understanding ethnography as a 'toolbox': use whatever you want – to start building whatever you feel like!

Mixing and matching? Picking a 'tool' for your project

As a caveat: while we like thinking about ethnography as a 'toolbox', and tools as always at least partially multifunctional and adaptable, you still cannot just randomly pick one. Finding the right tool, for your project is part of the research process:

1 *Not every ethnographic method fits with every topic.*
   Very intimate and personal practices, such as fandom for 'niche' objects like slash fiction (same-sex romantic fiction written by fans around beloved characters) for example, are difficult to discuss in a room full of strangers – as might happen with a focus group.
2 *Not every ethnographic method fits with every audience.*
   Interested in exploring how elderly residents of care homes decide what to watch next? You will probably not find them discussing this on social media.
3 *Not every ethnographic method fits with every researcher.*
   While it is important to think about the topic and the audience, you – the researcher – also play a role in deciding which methods work. For example, if you don't enjoy talking to strangers, interviews might not be the best method for you.

We hope you feel encouraged to try out various methods – and see which one works best for your topic, your audience and yourself. In different forms, ethnography returns in practice in several chapters: from collaborative autoethnography in *Chapter 10: "You knock on my door": An insider-Outsider View of Turkish Soap Operas and Fan Labor* via participant observation and focus groups in *Chapter 12: Sports Talk* to the long interview in *Chapter 14: Shared memories: Looking back at favorite teenage television*. In all of these case studies, drawing on ethnographic methods helped open up new paths to knowledge – and unlock data that matter.

Research example: identity, representation and the Hijabi on *Élite*

When the first episode of the second season of the Spanish teen drama *Élite* premiered on 6 September 2019, the outroar was almost immediate.

A key concern was the representation of a young Muslim woman, Nadia Shanaa, one of the main characters of the show. Initially, the series was praised for its nuanced depiction of contemporary Muslim identity. Then, it offered a 'makeover' scene in a club that shows Nadia take off her hijab to impress the boy she likes. On social media platforms, videos, comments and memes highlighted the absurdity of this stereotypical image of young Muslim women. No, they are not just waiting for a charming white knight to sweep them off their feet and persuade them to take off their hijab as a sign of their liberation. For her master thesis, Mariam Yassein explored how cultural knowledge regarding the hijab is shared, shaped and used in and through these online discussions of the show – and graciously allowed us to share her methodological steps with you here.

How to 'find' a topic: drawing on your own viewing experience

This is an example of a netnography that is partially connected to and inspired by autoethnography. Its topic and form of data collection are part of Mariam's biography as a viewer. She is not just a young audience researcher but also an avid and self-reflexive viewer of *Élite*. Set at an exclusive private school in Spain, the series plays with the clash between three working-class students (the character Nadia is one of them) and their overly wealthy peers. In addition to being great entertainment – there is murder, love and lots of drama – the show also spoke to Mariam on a personal level. As a member of the Muslim community and young woman wearing a hijab, both the representation of Nadia and the discussion of this mediated representation connect to questions of cultural citizenship and identity. The complexity of her own reactions to Nadia's storyline worked as a starting point to explore the negotiations within online Muslim communities. For your own research projects, your self-identification as a viewer, a fan, or a member of a community can also point you in the direction of your research project. Not being a viewer, a fan, or a member can work equally well, as long as you reflect on your own identity and preconceptions.

Where to find discussions: TV Time as form of media diary

Especially when you are thinking about online spaces to conduct your netnography, returning to platforms, forums or websites that you are familiar with makes your research a lot easier. Mariam used the website – and corresponding app – *TV Time* throughout her highschool years in the United Arab Emirates and frequently read and posted there about the series she was watching at the time. *TV Time* notifies users as soon as a new episode of their favorite show is available and allows viewers to react and add comments underneath each episode. In this regard, *TV Time* functions as a 'media diary' of sorts (something we will discuss in the following chapter in more detail). To allow for a clearer understanding of the changing reactions in parallel to the narrative, Mariam stored the audience comments under each episode separately. To map a broader online community beyond English-speaking audiences, the collected data also included comments posted in French and Arabic (two languages she speaks) as well as Turkish and Portuguese (for which she used Google Translate). Not all comments posted under the different episodes were relevant for her research. To be considered for the analysis, the comments needed to both discuss the specific character and be written by people who identified as Muslim. How do you know whether somebody is a Muslim or not in an online setting, though? Mariam decided on three different identifiers: the pseudonym used, the profile picture and self-identification in the comment.

Arabic names were easy to spot by a member of the Muslim community and specifically Islamic names (such as Mohammed for men) were used regularly. Profile pictures were also easy as hijabis would have pictures of themselves with a scarf or little avatars or cartoons wearing a headscarf. Islamic calligraphy photos last but not least were an identifier. It is a way of identifying within the community that helps people avoid exposing their identities online. If in their comments, people would also say: 'I'm muslim therefore my opinion on this Muslim character matters' that would clinch matters. Of course, Arab names are also used by Christian Arabs and by ex-Muslims. This did not much bother Mariam as these commenters are also in many ways part of the Muslim community and speak to central concerns. Would people say they are a Muslim to have their opinion heard about a favorite character without being one? Well, perhaps. The kind of comments exchanged does not however suggest that such a practice was common or that trolls were trying to make discussion of Nadia veer off course.

How to approach online discussion: community and contradictions

Belonging to the same ethnic, cultural or religious group does not necessarily mean having a unanimous viewpoint regarding interculturally controversial debates. Diversity within any community also means diverse – and potentially contradictory – responses. This goes for Muslim communities the same way it does for others. In the debate about Nadia, Mariam noticed two opposing fractions: one supporting Nadia abandoning her hijab, and the other going against it. However, approaching the comments from a 'pro and con' perspective would have been dismissive of the cultural discourse and practice that come with being an active member of the community. A bit too simplistic, this would overlook the complexity of the affect that brought about the different positions Muslim-identified viewers adopted within the debate. Instead, the netnographic approach revealed that Muslim viewers – whether they were supporting or opposing the representation of Nadia – approached the media text in a similar way but had profoundly different reactions and affective experiences. Viewers, it seemed, bounced from one affective response to the other. The events brought forth in each episode appeared to trigger them. In a circular logic of feeling attracted and repelled, they brought their own experiences into dialog with the media text and with each other, exemplifying what was called cultural citizenship as popular culture-afforded dialog in Chapter 2.

References

Chang, Heewon, Faith Wambura Ngunjiri, and Kathy-Ann C. Hernandez. 2013. *Collaborative Autoethnography*. Developing Qualitative Inquiry 8. Walnut Creek, CA: Left Coast Press.

Decker, Stephanie, and Alan McKinlay. 2020. "Archival Ethnography." In *The Routledge Companion to Anthropology and Business*, edited by Raza A. Mir and Anne-Laure Fayard. Routledge Companions in Business, Management and Marketing. New York, NY: Routledge.

Draper, Jan. 2015. "Ethnography: Principles, Practice and Potential." *Nursing Standard* 29 (36): 36–41. https://doi.org/10.7748/ns.29.36.36.e8937.

Drotner, Kirsten. 1994. "Ethnographic Enigmas: 'The Everyday' in Recent Media Studies." *Cultural Studies* 8 (2): 341–57. https://doi.org/10.1080/09502389400490491.

Gillespie, Marie. 1995. *Television, Ethnicity, and Cultural Change*. Comedia. London/New York: Routledge.

Glaw, Xanthe, Kerry Inder, Ashley Kable, and Michael Hazelton. 2017. "Visual Methodologies in Qualitative Research: Autophotography and Photo Elicitation Applied to Mental Health Research." *International Journal of Qualitative Methods* 16 (1): 160940691774821. https://doi.org/10.1177/1609406917748215.

Gray, Ann. 1992. *Video Playtime: The Gendering of a Leisure Technology*. Comedia. London/New York: Routledge.

Gray, Jonathan. 2021. *Dislike-Minded: Media, Audiences, and the Dynamics of Taste*. Critical Cultural Communication. New York: New York University Press.

Ihlebæk, Karoline Andrea, and Carina Riborg Holter. 2021. "Hostile Emotions: An Exploratory Study of Far-Right Online Commenters and Their Emotional Connection to Traditional and Alternative News Media." *Journalism* 22 (5): 1207–22. https://doi.org/10.1177/1464884920985726.

Livingstone, Sonia M., and Peter K. Lunt. 1994. *Talk on Television: Audience Participation and Public Debate*. Communication and Society. London/New York: Routledge.

Lull, James. 1988. *World Families Watch Television*. London: Sage.

Morley, David. 1999. *Family Television: Cultural Power and Domestic Leisure*. Reprinted. A Comedia Book. London: Routledge.

Schrøder, Kim Christian. 1994. "Audience Semiotics, Interpretive Communities and the 'Ethnographic Turn' in Media Research." *Media, Culture & Society* 16 (2): 337–47. https://doi.org/10.1177/016344379401600208.

Silverstone, Roger, Eric Hirsch, and David Morley. 1991 "Listening to a Long Conversation. An Ethnographic Approach to the Study of Information and Communication Technologies in the Home." *Cultural Studies* 5 (2): 204–27.

Steedman, Carolyn. 1986. *Landscape for a Good Woman: A Story of Two Lives*. London: Virago.

Thornton, Sarah. 1995. *Club Cultures*. Oxford: Polity Press.

Wood, Helen. 2017. "The Politics of Hyperbole on *Geordie Shore* : Class, Gender, Youth and Excess." *European Journal of Cultural Studies* 20 (1): 39–55. https://doi.org/10.1177/1367549416640552.

5 Audience-led analysis
Or: on how to be invited 'in'

Helen Wood cautions that analyzing television as 'text' "flattens the spatial and temporal experience of television as it takes place, *happens*, in the life of the living room" (2009, 4). Expanding on the introduction of ethnography-in-action in the previous chapter, we are approaching media practices as something intimate, something private here – and audience research as something that is all about being 'invited in'. Thinking about how media are always embedded in the everyday opens up to insights that go beyond the medium as 'text'. In other words, we are asking ourselves:

What can inviting audiences to talk about everyday media practices tell us about community, identity and intimacy?

Understanding how audiences consume, interact with and reflect on media objects leads us from open questions to more focused ones that help theorize findings. It means putting "human experience at the center of our inquiry" (2003, 174), as media and cultural studies scholar Jane Stokes proposed. Instead of emphasizing questions of objectivity versus subjectivity, using audience-led analysis means foregrounding reflexivity. In practice, this means reflecting on your own preconceptions and intuitive and instinctive reactions. You do so in order to remain open to hearing what others have to say. As a starting point for audience-led analysis, this chapter introduces you to Media Mapping, Media Diaries and Qualitative Interviews – three different approaches that work well alone but also in tandem.

Television and the everyday: talk me through your day

'Television studies' as a discipline pays attention to not just what's on television, but to the context of media consumption. Media, whether television or social media, are woven into the fabric of everyday life. As media change, our surroundings change and will 'feel' differently. Sonia

DOI: 10.4324/9781003315421-8

Livingstone (2007) has argued that the 'portability' of media, for example, changed life in the family home. Whereas the traditional television set constructed a communal space that family life centered around, smartphones, tablets, laptops and other 'personal media' devices are dispersed throughout the home and create a more and more individual media consumption. Anna McCarthy (2001) followed television outside of the home: in waiting rooms in hospitals, in the lobbies of airports and train stations, in laundromats, in bars and in the windows of different stores as some sort of 'ambient television'. In both of these seminal books, the presence of television or screens really is connected to questions of community and belonging.

As audience researchers, we are interested in these questions as well – and always hope to be 'invited in'. *When* and *where* you watch something might be as important, if not even more important, as *what* you watch. *What* you watch will depend on what you have access to financially and technologically, it might also depend on what you have in the fridge, how you travel to and from work or school, which device is currently charged, or when you have to get up in the morning. Being able to engage with audiences in their everyday allows us to explore these spatial, temporal, social, financial and technical dimensions of media practices.

Importantly, this means that we do not assume that audiences 'just' do what companies, corporations or larger commercial systems want them to do. In their exploration of 'roaming' audiences, Annette Hill and Jian Chung Lee (2022) were interested in how viewers in Malaysia and Indonesia move across streaming services – from Netflix to Youtube to public broadcasting channels and back to Netflix. To make visible how audiences navigate these different platforms, channels and services, they asked their participants to – literally – draw a map of their viewing practices. Interestingly, the participants in Hill and Lee's study drew on familiar types of maps and landscapes to think about what places and spaces different players and platforms occupied. *Disney* was described as a tall tower, *Netflix* as a commercial Business Park where not everything is accessible to everyone. Thinking about media in relation to their environment – be it real or fictional – can help audience researchers make sense of how viewers engage with different media throughout their day.

Practice exercise: mapping media

For this exercise, think about how you 'move' through, within and across different media platforms in the span of an average day: where are different media positioned on this map? What are the connections between different platforms and services? And what do different platforms look like?

Reflecting on the position, size and accessibility of different platforms, services and channels can tell you something about the different roles platforms play in your day. You might think differently about Netflix than you do about Public Broadcasting or torrent sites. You may feel that the world of media is changing and is offering less and less access to 'free' content. Or you might feel that the ways others operate on social media is spoiling the fun for the majority of okay users which is starting to make you hesitate to post comments, reactions or reflections yourself.

From one platform to another (and back again): the media diary

What do you watch on an average day? Are you consuming different media on a Tuesday then on a Sunday? Where and when do you use your smartphone the most? Asked out of the blue, these questions might actually not be that easy to answer. Exploring *when, where* and *how* audiences use different platforms – and different media on these platforms – has the potential to tell us a lot about how audiences come to terms with new forms, formats and rules on social media and professional content platforms in the cross-media landscape. As we are not scientists observing viewers in a laboratory, these everyday practices and sentiments can be difficult to track. Easiest to get your participants to track them for you. Enter: The 'Media Diary'. In their large study on changing news consumption, Nick Couldry, Sonia Livingstone and Tim Markham noticed that self-produced diaries "generated evidence about the context (social or otherwise) of everyday action that would not otherwise be available" (2007, 45). The 'Media Diary' tracks media practices as well as reflections about them – without the researcher having to be 'there'.

There is no predefined timeframe for making sense of viewing practices. There is no need for a particular moment to start or end your diary-keeping. Noting what you watch, where you watch it and what you notice about your own viewing practices over a longer period of time can reveal both patterns and changes. It can help you as a researcher and it potentially provides valuable material to the research community. Think, for example, how living with somebody else besides your family – like a partner or a roommate – has influenced your viewing habits. Do you 'wait' for each other to watch the newest episode of a series? Has owning a second device, like a smartphone or tablet, changed how you watch something on your laptop or on a big screen? What do you pay attention to, and how do the visuals and the sound become decoupled from another? Keeping a detailed viewing diary requires quite an effort. When you are asking others to keep track of their viewing, it can be a challenge to motivate your participants to keep going. We, therefore, recommend finding a 'happy' format: a media diary needs to be easy to fill out, carry with you, and be easy to remember. You can find a template that we use regularly in this chapter: rather than ask for long reflections, we prefer using a table-format that works well with quick note taking while watching or remembering something. For some, a simple notebook works best (Figure 5.1).

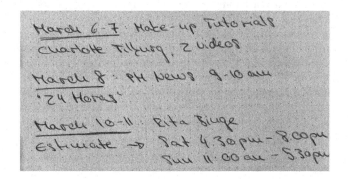

Figure 5.1

Anonymized fragment shared with permission from a media diary used in preparation for an interview about the current media landscape. By paying attention to your own 'micro' decisions, you start to see how much media content is used almost subconsciously and disappears from your thoughts easily. This does not mean that it is inconsequential. The make-up tutorial may have strengthened self-confidence for important life decisions, the binge may have allowed for working through whatever has been occupying the diary keeper. Media diaries just like this one help us to become attentive to the range of possible forms of media use to focus on in an ensuing interview.

In addition to 'new' media diaries, you can also find various already existing informal 'archives' of viewing habits and practices online. The website and app *TV Times* that we used as a research example in *Chapter 4: Ethnography* is also a 'viewing diary' of sorts: users are notified via the website/app as soon as a new episode of their favorite series is available. They can comment (and read comments) as soon as they have confirmed that they have watched the episode. Because of the availability of ratings, reviews and comments per episode, the process of watching-and-commenting becomes more immediate than on other platforms. That makes using *TV Times* more similar to a viewing diary than comments posted on Facebook, for instance. The audiovisual formats we discuss in *Chapter 6: Visual Analysis* can also involve a form of media tracking. An example are 'A Day in the Life' videos posted on Instagram. As a mini vlog documenting an average day, most of these videos will likely also involve media practices. Although they are highly edited, stylized and condensed, they can point you to what media habits and practices are common or considered desirable.

The 'media diary' works well combined with other qualitative methods, particularly with interviews. Talking about *what, why,* and *where* your respondents watched something does not only give you something to (start to) talk about in an interview but also reveals the preconceived notions of researchers and participants. Nick Couldry, Sonia Livingstone and Tim Markham call this "the subtle, sometimes conflicted ways in which information is processed, ideas mulled over and responses contemplated" (2007, 45).

Practice exercise: the media diary

For this exercise, try to 'record' your viewing practices in as much detail as possible – and ask yourself afterward what you might have missed. This becomes especially interesting when you compare your viewing diary to someone else's. Did you watch the same things, in the same environments, or at the same time?

Table 5.1

Day and Date	Time and Length	Platform Where did you watch this, i.e. on HBO Max, on Instagram?	Device What device did you watch this on, i.e. Phone, Laptop, Television?	Environment Where did you watch this, i.e. in your living room, on the bus, at university?	Program What did you watch, i.e. name of the series, Youtube channel?	Content What was happening in the program, i.e. the topic of the clip, the plot of the show?	Dialogue Did you watch this together with someone, or chat about it? Before, during or after? In person or on a platform?	Comments/Questions

From 'my' day to 'your' day: qualitative interviews

To make sense of viewing practices, self-recording tools like maps and media diaries will not tell you everything you want (or need) to know. Media diaries made during the Covid-19 pandemic showed how viewing practices had profoundly changed. The evening news on broadcast television became an important source for information about new rules and regulations. As did livestreamed press conferences that most of us – under ordinary circumstances – would not have watched. Television had again become a medium of 'liveness', somewhat surprising in an increasingly fractured and on-demand media landscape. To further explore the corresponding question "How did the *meaning* of television viewing change during the pandemic?" you would need the people who filled them out.

For interviews, there are a few logistical questions to consider: first and foremost *where* to find participants, *what* to ask them and *how* to conduct your interview.

1   *The Where: Finding Your Participants*

Once you know that you want to do interviews, you likely want to get started right away. But who to interview? Depending on your subject, you could start in your immediate surroundings. Your family members, your roommates, your friends and your fellow students make great participants for your first interviews. They already know and trust you. You can also easily remind them of the scheduled interviews! These first interviewees might then be able to recommend somebody else for you to talk to. This is called 'snowballing'. Their family members, their roommates, their friends and their fellow students are called 'seeds'. When used well, the danger of remaining in your own 'bubble' is manageable. It is a matter of instructing the 'seed' persons well. Interestingly, methodologists have found that snowballing runs the risk of overselecting women. They are assumed to be more cooperative and less able to resist a researcher's request' (Noy 2008). As women, we are not so sure this will be the case. As feminists, we caution you to be aware of such social power mechanisms, which will also be related to, e.g., class, educational level and ethnicity.

Of course, you can also start with an open call for participants. Ien Ang, in her groundbreaking study of *Watching Dallas*, placed an ad in the Dutch women's magazine *Viva* to find respondents. Quite importantly, she positioned herself as a frequent viewer of the American soap herself and asked: "Would anyone like to write and tell me why you like watching it too, or dislike it?" (1985, 10). Today's version of placing a newspaper ad could be a post on your Instagram Story. Based on a very, very short summary of your research idea, you can ask your friends and followers to share your open call as well in order to find research participants from outside your own circle of family, friends and acquaintances. While you can find plenty of useful advice for online snowball methods, changing privacy regulations make these more difficult to employ: the option of randomly approaching others on social media has more and more closed down. Our advice is to be patient and tenacious. It will require time to find (enough) participants. Be persistent in following up with people who agreed to participate, they tend to cancel interview appointments last-minute. Do not let yourself be discouraged!

2 *The What: Structuring Your Interviews*
As we have discussed in *Chapter 4: Ethnography*, an interview allows you to directly follow up on what your participants say. 'Follow up' to clarify answers, yes. But also to literally 'follow' your participants – in directions and toward topics that you might not have anticipated. That said: you still need to have a structure for your interview. Especially for new audience researchers, going into an interview without a plan rarely goes well. You might run out of questions or lose track of what you were actually interested in. In between a strict order of questions and no order at all, is the 'semi-structured interview'. In practice, this means that you prepare not necessarily questions but conversation topics that you want to touch on in each interview. This allows the conversation to flow freely, and your participants to be involved in the direction the conversation can go in. At the same time, the topic list in front of you (or in the back of your mind) helps you steer the conversation back on course when you want to. As you talk to more participants, you might also want to go back to your topic list and revise it based on previous interviews. This process of gradually focusing the research is a strength of qualitative research. It allows embracing unfolding insight. In quantitative research, such a procedure is anathema. It hopelessly upsets the possibility of pure comparison. Fortunately, that is not what we are interested in.

3 *The How: Being an Interviewer*
When you are asking your participants about everyday practices, it helps to see them as *experts*. Even if you are doing the exact same things in your leisure time, if you have watched the same shows, played the same games or hated the same character, you want to know how *they* (!) do and feel. While shared interests and experiences help to find participants and get them to talk to you in the first place, the interview situation itself places the focus on the participant. In practice, this means that you draw on the expertise of your participants to ask for definitions, for explanations, for contextualization. You do not impose your own. When you read the transcripts of interviews

conducted by others, you will see that good interviewers know how to follow-up on what their participants say. They are genuinely curious about how their participants make sense of and find meaning in their everyday practices. Sometimes, you might want to slightly 'push' your respondent's buttons – by offering an alternative understanding of a scene or a news item, for instance, or by asking for an evaluation of a statement. You do not do this to catch them out. Rather, you are trying to get access to the varied ways in which they make sense of the world.

Jonathan Potter and Margaret Wetherell (1988) underline how language is both functional and variable and that this allows us in everyday conversations to not always be consistent. Rather than see this as lying, or misrepresentation, the use of different 'interpretative repertoires' points to the different cultural resources we have for sense and meaning-making. Social beings that we are, we will use whatever resources we ourselves have available to connect with the knowledge of others in a conversation. As researchers, we like to make friendly use of this mechanism. When we challenge informants with questions like: "Is this fair, though?" or "Would you really do this?", we are carefully inviting respondents to think about their statements and offer further explanation. You want to avoid aggressive or presumptuous questions. This might not need repeating but still: as an interviewer your main task is to be open and respectful. To listen to what others have to say.

Research example: 'as recommended by' and the trust in technology

Netflix, Amazon, Youku, Disney, Ziggo, Tencent, Hulu, iflix – the number of streaming platforms becomes longer and longer. How do you decide what to watch (next)? With new content premiering across platforms constantly, professional television critics can hardly keep up with everything that needs to be reviewed and 'judged' for a comprehensive recommendation – especially as it comes to global shows and series. Cue 'protoprofessionalization', as Jan Teurlings (2018) calls it. Because of the narrow scope of professional reviews, new recommendation and suggestion systems are on the rise: from community-based recommendations like ratings on online forums such as *Rotten Tomatoes* via the integrated algorithmic recommendations à la "Suggested for you" on different streaming platforms to interpersonal recommendations by people viewers know outside of the digital world. For a small-scale project, we were interested in how viewers navigate these different sources of recommendations. Whose recommendations are the most trustworthy? Is there a difference between human and nonhuman, offline and online recommendations? Because these are complex questions directly linked to practices and the reasoning behind these practices, we decided to conduct long interviews.

The participants: how do you decide who to interview?

In the selection of interviewees for this example, we considered three markers: age, gender and place of residence. As Oblak and Luther have argued, contemporary audience research should take social markers like the ones mentioned above into account, as they "provide a framework of meaning for [...] media consumption and interpretation" (2017, 419). At the same time, there are many more markers – so why these three? *Age and Gender*: We decided to interview young women of the same age group between 29 and 35 years. Born in the mid to late 1980s, this age group can be considered what Palfrey and Gasser term the first generation of digital natives (2008). Based on age, we assumed that our participants would be familiar with similar platforms and (online) tools and share at least some media practices in their daily lives. *Gender*: especially as it comes to the targeting of advertisements, gender plays an important role. Using gender as our marker here as well allowed us to explore whether our participants noticed similar recommendations given to them in online and offline settings. *Place of Residence*: as the (perceived) size of available content can differ immensely between different platforms and countries, we chose participants based on their access to a specific – and national – platform. All three interviewees have or previously had a place of residence in Germany, and thereby access to Netflix in Germany in addition to possible other platforms. Having one local(ized) platform as a reference point shifted the attention away from platform-specific factors like performance or interface design. As you can see from this brief overview, all decisions – even as it comes to who to interview – need to be thought about carefully and justified.

The questions: how do you decide what to ask?

The conversation topics for this project were (1) *Recommendations*: where do viewers notice recommendations – and do they follow them?, (2) *Conversations*: with whom and where did viewers discuss what they have (not) watched? and (3) *Technologies*: how do viewers understand the role of different platforms in their decisions and conversations? For each of these topics, we prepared questions and/ or points to bring up. After each interview, we updated these lists with input from the participants – to then, in turn, draw on these in the next interview. As a starting point, we asked each participant what they had watched 'last' – and what made them start this show in the first place. During the interview, we placed different sources of recommendations as opposites. Not only in terms of their trust-worthiness but also their effectiveness. Questions like: "Do you trust the recommendations of your friends more than online recommendations?" or "Does the algorithm predict your taste better than your friends?" were meant to access feelings about technology. Each interview ended in a similar way: by asking our participants whether they recommended media to other people – and why (not). Circling back to the question of personal recommendations at the end of the interview allowed the participants to reflect on practices of decision-making as passive 'receiver' and active 'giver' of recommendations. It also allowed them to expand on and add to earlier answers.

The answers: how do you decide what's the most important?

In the answers, we began to notice that 'trust' played an important role for our participants. It also clearly intersected with how they thought about technology. Moving beyond our research question: "How do you decide what to watch?", the qualitative interviews pointed us to how viewers navigate the technologization of television in a cross-media landscape. On the one hand, respondents embraced the convenience afforded by technological solutions; on the other hand, they all emphasized their distrust in the intentions behind these exact technological affordances. At first, these two repertoires appear to be contradictory. Taken together, they produce a sense of 'comfort' for the respondents that has often been associated with watching television in general. The convenience afforded by technological recommendations provides a comfortable simplification in an already complicated world full of choices. For digital natives like our respondents, it was equally comforting to suggest they understood the 'hidden' workings of technologies like the algorithms used by online video platforms. By acknowledging the manipulation, the respondents felt they could negate its (potentially harmful) influence. It justified giving in to the convenience of using untrustworthy technology. This is a direction we did not expect when we started out with this case study – but one that we found highly interesting. This is something that might happen in your interviews too: following your participants might lead you to find unexpected answers as well as new insights.

Exercise: template for your interview form

Name interviewer	
Name respondent (Pseudonym)	
Date interview	
Location interview	
Duration interview (00.00 – 00.00)	
Age respondent	
Gender	
Sexual orientation	
Class background	
Residence	
Composition of household	
National identification	
Political preference	
Work, study	
Way of living/lifestyle	
Consent Form Signed	[ ] YES [ ] NO
Remarks	

To be filled out by the interviewer – Observation remarks (verbal, non-verbal, atmosphere, interruptions during the interview, etc.)

References

Ang, Ien. 1985. *Watching Dallas: Soap Opera and the Melodramatic Imagination*. London: Routledge.

Couldry, Nick, Sonia M. Livingstone, and Tim Markham. 2007. *Media Consumption and Public Engagement: Beyond the Presumption of Attention*. Consumption and Public Life. Basingstoke, Hampshire/New York: Palgrave Macmillan.

Hill, Annette, and Jian Chung Lee. 2022. "Roamers: Audiences on the Move Across Entertainment Platforms in Southeast Asia." *Javnost - The Public* 29 (1): 98–114. https://doi.org/10.1080/13183222.2021.1932985.

Livingstone, Sonia M. 2007. "From Family Television to Bedroom Culture: Young People's Media at Home." In *Media Studies: Key Issues and Debates*, edited by Eoin Devereux, 302–21. London: SAGE Publications.

McCarthy, Anna. 2001. *Ambient Television: Visual Culture and Public Space*. Console-Ing Passions. Durham: Duke University Press.

Noy, Chaim. 2008. "Sampling Knowledge: The Hermeneutics of Snowball Sampling in Qualitative Research." *International Journal of Social Research Methodology* 11 (4), 327–44. https://doi.org/10.1080/13645570701401305.

Oblak Črnič, Tanja, and Breda Luthar. 2017. "Media Repertoires and Discursive Communities: Studying Audiences in the Multimedia Age." *Communications* 42 (4). https://doi.org/10.1515/commun-2017-0028.

Palfrey, John, and Urs Gasser. 2008. *Born Digital: Understanding the First Generation of Digital Natives*. New York: Basic Books.

Potter, John, and Margaret Wetherell. 1988. "Discourse Analysis and the Identification of Interpretative Repertoires." In *Analysing Everyday Explanation: A Casebook of Methods*, 168–83. London: Sage Publications.

Stokes, Jane C. 2003. *How to Do Media & Cultural Studies*. London/Thousand Oaks, CA: SAGE.

Teurlings, Jan. 2018. "Social Media and the New Commons of TV Criticism." *Television & New Media* 19 (3): 208–24. https://doi.org/10.1177/1527476417709599.

Wood, Helen. 2009. *Talking with Television: Women, Talk Shows, and Modern Self-Reflexivity*. Feminist Studies and Media Culture. Urbana: University of Illinois Press.

6 Visual analysis
Or: how images and words 'mean' together

As researchers interested in everyday meaning-making, we need to take into account what Fiske (1987) called primary and secondary texts – which include television, films, books or trailers and reviews in newspapers – as well as tertiary texts – which include audiences talking about all of these. Rather than understand these types of sources as individual and insular, we propose that images and words 'mean' together. And that there is something to be gained from not only a multisource but a multimethod approach.

How can visual analysis be understood as complementary to and part of audience research?

Stepping away from 'talking' to and with audiences as we did in the previous chapter, here, we want to focus on affect and sensory appeal as reconstructed in visual analysis. What happens when we start with the text rather than the audience? Can it be done? Or is there a great risk of academic knowledge and analysis overshadowing everyday meaning-making?

Audience researchers need to critically assess how they use *visual analysis*, *textual analysis* or *narrative analysis*. As has been argued in the preceding chapters: it is easy to suggest that 'The Researcher Knows Better'. Sometimes you really might. But most of the time, privileging your own interpretation has the risk of drowning out what others might be seeing, hearing, sensing. And that, ultimately, means that you are missing out on unexpected perspectives and findings. As a disclaimer: in our version of doing visual analysis, the audience is still present. After all, you are a viewer as well as a researcher. The shared meanings created in and through media that we discussed in the first chapters of this book return here: the 'text' itself becomes a shared resource that audiences draw on, reflect on and think about in their everyday lives. This chapter

DOI: 10.4324/9781003315421-9

will present textual analysis as part of an assemblage in which audience attachments play an important role. Or, as Gillian Rose put it: "Images circulate, then, but they also land in specific places, where they are seen by people: Their audiences" (2016, 38). Only in our attachments (as audience members and as professional researchers) are specific meanings 'activated'. Pointing to the connections between the visuals and their embodied experience opens up new ways of understanding meaning-making across different media forms.

Watching and/as talking: media research as assemblage

One of the words that comes up in relation to media across different contexts is 'assemblage': Based on the work of philosophers Gilles Deleuze and Félix Guattari, this means that the material and immaterial sides of media work together – and can constantly change. As an assemblage of technologies, people and meanings, media are not static and stable. And neither is how we think and feel about them! In this chapter, we want to suggest understanding methodology as an assemblage as well. Something that depends on the moment, and the perspective. Something that changes once we add new elements. In her work on television talk shows, Helen Wood has simultaneously recorded both the television programs itself and the viewer responses as they watch shows like *Oprah*, "making visible television viewings as a communicative event" (2009, 5). Communication can also always go multiple ways. In other courses, you might have come across Stuart Hall's definition of 'reading positions'. In his Encoding/Decoding model, a media text – a film, the news, a television show – is constructed by the producers and encoded with an intended meaning (Hall 2003). Other than in a sender-message-receiver model, the audience plays an active role in then decoding that message.

This can potentially go multiple ways, which doesn't mean that 'every individual just interprets differently' but rather that the codes we used are not universal but dependent on other factors such as time, education, sociocultural context and so on. Some viewers will follow the 'preferred meaning' of the text as it has been encoded. Others will make a 'negotiated' reading in which they accept some but not all of the preferred meaning. Still others will engage in an 'oppositional' reading, not only disagreeing with the preferred meaning, but also recognizing its ideological nature and role in justifying power relations and established norms.

Thinking visual analysis together with other methods also has the potential to point us to the contradictions in media practices. An approach that "serves collective knowledge building and reflexivity, the training of future professionals and 'maker knowledge'" (Hermes

Visual analysis = textual analysis?

Throughout this chapter, we use the terms visual analysis and textual analysis interchangeable, which can be a bit confusing at first. In media studies, 'text' does not (only) mean the written word. For our research, all sorts of media become texts to be read and interpreted: films, television, social media posts, advertising, art installations and so on. Some of these are 'texts' in the more classic sense, some of these are only visual, some are both. Especially in a cross-mediated landscape, texts might also change and shift. Think, for example, about the pilot of a new television show that is reviewed by an online magazine and shared in edited snippets on social media. Media researchers might be interested in either of these – or all three. What's important is understanding that media can be analyzed in all of their forms through different methods.

A great starting point to dive further into visual analysis is Gillian Rose's *"Visual Methodologies: An Introduction to Researching with Visual Materials"* (2016).

2024). Starting from the text, and from our own enjoyment (or committed hatred), functions as a way to center ourselves as both researchers and viewers. The 'and' is very important here: researchers are trained to be critical, to be objective, to be distant. With that, occasionally, comes a tendency to look at media texts from above, from a position of knowledge and power and authority. Highlighting that we are always researchers *and* viewers aims to counter this. It asks us to be reflective and to understand how our own experiences of and with media inform our analysis of ethnographic materials. Christine Geraghty put it beautifully bluntly: media studies would benefit from "academics being more explicit about the evaluative judgements that we inevitably make" (2003, 40). These judgments become particularly visible when you do a textual analysis together with someone else – a collaborative textual analysis, of sorts.

Joke Hermes writes about this in *Cultural Citizenship* (2024): Watching the crime drama *The Mentalist* with different family members. Originally, a broadcast series on the US network *CBS*, the narrative centered on 'psychic' Patrick Jane and his consulting work for the California Bureau of Investigation is now available on a variety of streaming platforms. Reruns of the show (which ended after seven seasons and 151 episodes in 2018) still come up on cable television again and again. Watching and rewatching a series like this can attune you to different elements. You might start to realize that you are paying attention to different things than the people you are (re)watching the show with. From the main character's fashion sense to his very hipster modes of transportation in the series to the construction of the police department as a 'work family': it turns out that the text tells different stories at the same time. 'Just' doing textual analysis might not pick up on this. For film studies, but also in more traditional television research, textual analysis is often geared toward reconstructing the one deeper meaning of a text. Exploring the visual and narrative dimension of the series together with our own perspectives as viewers – and in conversation with other viewers – points us to its multiple (rather than its deeper) meanings. Thinking of different methods together is the goal here. Sometimes, as in the example above, this might mean to quite literally do a visual analysis as a form of collaborative ethnographic exploration. At other times, this might mean starting from an analysis of interview materials or other audience data to then turn to the text itself to understand the responses as part of a broader pattern.

Exercise: reacting to reactions on TikTok

If reactions are becoming more visual, we might also want to analyze them visually. For this exercise, look up reactions to one of your most recent favorite television shows on TikTok. A good starting point for this is a search using "Name of the Show" and the keyword "Reaction" – this also works if you do not have an account on the social media platform. Especially if your example is fairly popular with other viewers as well, this search should quickly give you a list of reaction videos to potentially look at. As you start to click through them, pay attention to the visual elements:

> *How is the original show integrated into the reaction video? Can you see the screen where the show is playing? Is the reaction shown next to the original content in a 'stitch'? Or is the focus solely on the person reacting? What else can you see and hear besides the show and the person reacting to it?*

Paying attention to these elements in a visual analysis can help you to move beyond the 'content' of the reaction videos (i.e., whether the person reacting feels the same way about the show as you do).

Instead, the visual analysis might point you to other questions that could be interesting to explore as it comes to your favorite television show – from which scenes and moments were particularly featured (and why that might be) to shared viewing practices (and what that might mean).

Research example: reality television through and beyond the text

There is another research project by Helen Wood that we very much enjoyed – which perfectly shows how different methods can come together to paint a larger picture. In "The Politics of Hyperbole on *Geordie Shore*: Class, Gender, Youth and Excess", Helen Wood interprets statements from the participants of the British reality television show *Geordie Shore*, their visual appearance as well the production process and aesthetics of the show itself in a qualitative research model. By interpreting conversations and statements from the show's participants throughout different seasons, Wood focuses on the self-portrayal and self-identification of the cast. She does more, however. She takes into account statements made by the participants 'in' the episodes, but also 'outside' of the filming of the reality television show, for instance, in interviews with the British newspaper *The Daily Mirror* and the online news site *Huffington Post*.

In addition to analyzing the verbal statements of the participants of '*Geordie Shore*', Wood uses visual descriptions of the participants, for example "*all of the women have excessively long 'mermaid' hair extensions, extended false finger nails, eyelashes, high-definition and exaggerated eyebrows, some breast augmentation and deep orange tans*" (2017, 45). This visual description provides further context to the verbal statements and functions as an additional layer in how particular identities are produced. Not just the visual appearance of the participants but also the aesthetics of the show itself – in the sense of the production and editing process – are drawn into the analysis to focus on the contrast between the showing *of* the actual scene and the commentary *about* the scene. By using expressions like "*in which the kinetic editing of the scene and the commentary exaggerate the act as comedic cartoon*" (Wood 2017, 48), "*we see edited clips of her stumbling [...], which are then put together*", "*... much goes into its frenetic* *(hyper) animation*" (Wood 2017, 40). Wood emphasizes the framing and forming done by television. Individually, the statements of the participants on and off the show, the visual analysis of their appearance or the textual analysis of the show would have certainly been interesting. Once they are taken together, the argument of 'hyperbolic framing' becomes truly convincing.

'Sensing' media: meaning-making as embodied practice

In this book, we have offered you different definitions of ethnography, and particularly media ethnography, before – but we would like to add one more: ethnography as an iterative and interactive "process of creating and representing knowledge that is based on the ethnographer's own experience and the ways these experiences intersect with persons, places and things encountered during that process" (Pink 2015, 5). Ethnography is a way of creating knowledge that involves the ethnographer – you – and others, in some sort of interaction. Shifting the focus from the interaction itself to how this interaction feels, how we experience persons, places and things – including media – brings us to a new cross-media dimension related to our senses. Research can be based on more than facts and figures! When we start paying attention to how we experience media through our senses, we are opening up to wider discussion of media examples. In *Chapter 2*, we introduced you to the term 'affect' – and it is a useful term to return to here. "People's knowledge of themselves, others and the world they inhabit, is inextricably linked to and shaped by their senses", writes Andrew Sparkes (2009, 23). Thinking about how a media text makes you *feel*, how it appeals to your senses as much as your sensibilities can help make clear how and why we are attached to it which otherwise might well remain a bit of a mystery. Rita Felski has addressed this in her books *The Limits of Critique* (2015) and *Hooked* (2020).

The affective dimensions of media especially play a role in 'charged' contexts. The international soccer tournaments we discuss in Chapter 12, for instance, or the hate/love relationship viewers might have with complex characters and ambiguous storylines in fictional dramas like we discuss in *Chapter 8* on the Netflix drama *You*. In these examples, what's happening on the screen and what's happening in front of it are connected. You might jump up as 'your' team scores. You might cringe as the main character of *You* utters another romantic-yet-creepy line. You might laugh because the person sitting next to you is laughing. All of these examples are affect in action. They make visible how media, quite literally, do something to us. As both researcher *and* viewer, you are in a unique position to explore this tension between the text itself and its sensory experience.

Exercise: sensing without thinking

Especially if you are used to analyzing and interpreting, 'sensing' can seem a bit nonsensical. But this is exactly what this exercise challenges you to do: to sense without thinking, to feel without evaluating. This works easiest when you draw on your own memory of a media object that you have not watched (too) recently: What are the images that immediately come to your mind? Which character do you think of first? Which colors do you associate with this media object? And what do you feel when thinking back to the first (or last) time you watched this? Finding out about your own associative meanings before entering into analytical mode can help attune you to specific elements and narratives within the text as well as evaluations and judgments you harbor about them.

For Christine Geraghty, this means "to make a very common, everyday process strange, and an emphasis on expression as well as meaning, on agency as well as representation, might provide different ways of looking at familiar material" (2003, 40). Here, we will turn to a type of material that might seem all too familiar – and is yet frequently overlooked in analysis. Advertising! To really catch our attention, advertising increasingly plays with our emotions. Timothy Malefyt proposes that "sentiment has become the ultimate consumer target by which new forms of media and brand messaging will shape and recast consumers' sensory and emotional experiences" (2007, 231). With the 'sensorial turn', advertising moves away from information and reason to appeal to our senses, to create an embodied experience for us as viewers, users, consumers. Emotions reign. This is also something that you can see in most of the ads surrounding you both on and off the screen: Advertisers have begun to take a less general 'rational' approach by marketing to consumers with targeted messages through specific media that are more personalized, customized and sensory-engaging.

This experience is happening everywhere around us, all the time. Advertising might be the ultimate cross-media form – reaching us, touching our everyday lives through so many different forms. Classic print ads, sponsored stories on Instagram, city branding, posters, YouTube pre-rolls and other audiovisual ads... we might not even always notice the advertising around us. And yet, advertising is both part of culture and creating culture (Sheffield 2006). Because we are constantly surrounded by advertising, wherever we are, whatever we do, we also experience advertising's messages wherever we are, whatever we do. How do we make 'sense' of advertising, then? Asking ourselves how the sensorial appeal of advertisements informs and influences the understanding of different narratives also connects to larger questions of inclusion and exclusion, of participation and belonging.

Research example: "Alexa, help the baby sleep!"

In her research on imaginations of artificial intelligence, Linda Kopitz (2021) uses the visual analysis of four advertisements for the digital voice assistant *Amazon Alexa* as a starting point to explore the dynamics between technology and humans. All four commercials portray family dynamics – between mother, father and daughter; between a male caretaker and an elderly patient (supposedly) suffering from dementia; between a father and his newborn; and between a father and his daughter over the course of her childhood. Just from this list, it might seem like these ads are offering modern and alternative narratives of masculinity and fatherhood. At a closer look, however, these commercials return to traditional norms and expectations, especially as it comes to parenting. Presented as explicitly nonthreatening in its ordinariness, positive potential and gendered presence, the digital voice assistant becomes a member of the family – and more precisely, takes over the role of caring mother. One example: settling on the couch with the fidgeting baby, the young father turns toward Alexa with the exclamation "Alexa, help the baby sleep". This request splits the parenting role between the father and Alexa as a substitute for the absent mother. Although the command seems to be rather vague, the Alexa-enabled device reacts with something that could almost be seen as maternal instinct – by putting on a lullaby that immediately calms the baby down. Drawing on ethnographic data, Porcheron et al. have discussed the use of intelligent personal assistants – which would also include Amazon's Alexa – in multiparty conversations. According to their findings, users in social settings "collectively reorganize their body orientation around the device interaction, they pause their talk, they gaze at the tablet, and they attend to the answer as soon as it is provided" (Porcheron et al. 2017, 215). The notion of bodily reorientation and adaption of new conversational patterns – including a pause to implicitly allow the algorithm to provide the corresponding answer to the command, comes also through in the visual analysis of the four advertisements. In turn, the ease and ordinariness of these encounters with Alexa might also inform how we think about artificial intelligence in the home more generally – which is exactly where further audience research on these devices picks up from the visual analysis.

Google is an interesting example here: the company itself conducted an overview of their own marketing materials (2019) – and found the trends showing that some groups of people were being left out or misrepresented. For example, women had less speaking time, Black people were often portrayed in overused clichés like playing sports or dancing, and Latinos and people with disabilities were severely underrepresented across all materials. Through the visual analysis of these materials, a pattern of inclusion/exclusion became visible – which then formed the first steps toward doing things differently. Gillian Rose calls this "the grounding of interpretations of visual materials in careful empirical research of the social circumstances in which they are embedded" (2016, xxi).

Engaging with visual media can also come in the form of creating visual media: David Gauntlett, for example, discusses how images can function "as a way of exploring their relationship with particular issues or dimensions of media" (2005, 1). In some ways, we could understand this as an expansion of the media diaries and media maps we used as conversation starters in *Chapter 5*. In the following exercise on 'inclusive' advertising, we are bringing together sensory ethnography, visual analysis and 'prototyping' to not just see but change ads.

Exercise: all inclusive? Advertising in the city

How does the sensorial appeal of advertisement inform and influence our understanding of different narratives? This practice exercise maps the current state of advertising around you – before trying to imagine more inclusive alternatives based on your analysis.

1 *Collecting: which ads do you encounter where on an average day?*
   The starting point for this practice exercise is to – consciously – note the advertising around you. This works best if you define

a set time span to sense how different forms of ads surround you. For instance, by documenting every ad you encounter on your way from your home to university or your workplace. Try to pay attention to billboards, posters, screens, images in store-front windows, branded objects and take pictures that show the ad and its surroundings (no close-ups). To think about the cross-mediality of advertising, try to catalog the different forms of ads that might come up on your own devices as well. Did you scroll on social media while waiting for the bus? Take a screenshot of the sponsored content you are seeing! Did you listen to a music streaming service while cycling? Try to note the promotional breaks and interruptions! To really explore adver-tising in the city, we recommend that you plan at least 30 more minutes than you would normally need for the way. If you have extra time left, purposely get lost – make a detour, take a new street, and document the ads you encounter there. Of course, you can also repeat this data collection on different routes or combine your photos with those of your friends or peers com-ing from different parts of the city (or with different modes of transportation).

2   *Reviewing: what do you notice in your collected materials?*
What did you notice, what struck you as important, how did you experience their placement, had you noticed them before? What are you paying attention to and when? Tuning in to ad-vertising, as you have done in the first step, does more than al-low you to see your surroundings differently. It can also point you to different ways of living and knowing through the senses. As researchers, instead of just describing a place, we ask our-selves how we experience places and spaces – and how that in-forms our relationship to that place. This also has implications for you as researchers and (future) professionals – especially if you are interested in a career in advertising and similar creative industries. If you understand the everyday realities of people's experiences and practices, you are in position to also directly address and appeal to these experiences. Of course, the same goes for more activist approaches – how to create more inclu-sive spaces, for example. Paying attention to the senses moves design and artistic interventions away from an attempt to 'change' behavior, to think about how interventions can create

a positive, productive contribution to making and remaking sense and meaning in the everyday. And this is exactly what the next step asks you to do!

3 *Creative Prototyping: how can we reimagine advertising to be more inclusive?*
How we understand the world is very much connected to our senses as well, how we experience things, how we feel things. This, in turn, has implications to how we might intervene in the world – as researchers, as artists, as activists, as creative professionals. As a form of engaging differently with your collected materials, the next step in this exercise is to get creative. To prototype! And even if "you might not think of yourself as a designer, the chances are that you design every day" (Kimbell 2012, 5). Take a look at the collected materials through the thematic lens of your own experience: Who is being addressed, who is being included or excluded? And if you were in charge, how would you do this differently? For your prototype, you can either start with one of the images you took and improve from there, or you can start from scratch. Don't get caught up in your design skills, or the aesthetics. You can do this on paper by cutting out, pasting and drawing. You can do this on your computer in a document, a presentation or by overlaying one of the existing images. You can turn to design programs like Canva or InDesign. More important for this exercise is your appeal to the senses and the audiences you are addressing.

As a final step, place your reimagined ads next to the originals you photographed on your way through the city. Design thinker and researcher Lucy Kimbell refers to all of the materials around us as *stories, skills* and *stuff* (2011, 2012) to emphasize that what we see and do is always open to reimagination and recreation. Reflexivity – in the sense of thinking about what you sense and what that means – challenges your own practice and ideas and perceptions. As a crucial element to sensorial ethnography, your own creative practice and audience research more broadly, being able to switch perspectives and – literally and metaphorically – tune in to media and media practices around you will make you a better researcher. And it will hopefully make you (even) more aware of the role media plays in shaping the world around us.

References

Fiske, John. 1987. *Television Culture*. London ; New York: Methuen.

Gauntlett, David. 2005. "Using Creative Visual Research Methods to Understand Media Audiences." *MedienPädagogik: Zeitschrift Für Theorie und Praxis der Medienbildung* 9 (Visuelle Methoden): 1–32. https://doi.org/10.21240/mpaed/09/2005.03.29.X.

Geraghty, Christine. 2003. "Aesthetics and Quality in Popular Television Drama." *International Journal of Cultural Studies* 6 (1): 25–45. https://doi.org/10.1177/1367877903006001002.

Hall, Stuart. 2003. "Encoding/Decoding*." In *Culture, Media, Language*, edited By Stuart Hall, Dorothy Hobson, Andrew Lowe, Paul Willis, 117–27. London: Routledge.

Hermes, Joke. 2024. *Cultural Citizenship and Popular Culture. The Art of Listening*. London: Routledge.

Kimbell, Lucy. 2011. "Rethinking Design Thinking: Part I." *Design and Culture* 3 (3): 285–306. https://doi.org/10.2752/175470811X13071166525216.

———. 2012. "Rethinking Design Thinking: Part II." *Design and Culture* 4 (2): 129–48. https://doi.org/10.2752/175470812X13281948975413.

Kimbell, Lucy, and Joe Julier. 2012. "THE SOCIAL DESIGN METHODS MENU." http://www.lucykimbell.com/stuff/Fieldstudio_SocialDesignMethods Menu.pdf.

Kopitz, Linda. 2021. "Alexa, Affect, and the Algorithmic Imaginary: Addressing Privacy and Security Concerns Through Emotional Advertising." *Screen Bodies* 6 (1): 1–17. https://doi.org/10.3167/screen.2021.060103.

Malefyt, Timothy de Waal. 2007. "From Rational Calculation to Sensual Experience The Marketing of Emotions in Advertising." In *The Emotions: A Cultural Reader*, edited by Helena Wulff, 321–38. Oxford: Berg.

Pink, Sarah. 2015. *Doing Sensory Ethnography*. Second edition. London/Thousand Oaks, California: Sage Publications.

Porcheron, Martin, Joel E. Fischer, and Sarah Sharples. 2017. "'Do Animals Have Accents?': Talking with Agents in Multi-Party Conversation." In *Proceedings of the 2017 ACM Conference on Computer Supported Cooperative Work and Social Computing - CSCW '17*, 207–19. Portland, Oregon, USA: ACM Press. https://doi.org/10.1145/2998181.2998298.

Rose, Gillian. 2016. *Visual Methodologies: An Introduction to Researching with Visual Materials*. 4th ed. London: SAGE Publications Ltd.

Sheffield, Tricia. 2006. *The Religious Dimensions of Advertising*. 1st ed. Religion/Culture/Critique. New York: Palgrave Macmillan.

Sparkes, Andrew C. 2009. "Ethnography and the Senses: Challenges and Possibilities." *Qualitative Research in Sport and Exercise* 1 (1): 21–35. https://doi.org/10.1080/19398440802567923.

Twohill, Lorraine. 2019. "9 Ways We're Changing Habits, so We Can Make More Inclusive Marketing at Google." Think with Google. 2019. https://www.thinkwithgoogle.com/future-of-marketing/management-and-culture/diversity-and-inclusion/diversity-gender-inclusion-marketing/.

Wood, Helen. 2009. *Talking with Television: Women, Talk Shows, and Modern Self-Reflexivity*. Feminist Studies and Media Culture. Urbana: University of Illinois Press.

———. 2017. "The Politics of Hyperbole on Geordie Shore: Class, Gender, Youth and Excess." *European Journal of Cultural Studies* 20 (1): 39–55. https://doi.org/10.1177/1367549416640552.

7 Theorization
Or: how to get from data to theory

According to Lyn and Tom Richards (1994), the overriding goal of doing qualitative research (and the reason to prefer it over quantitative research) is that it *aids theory construction*. In this chapter, we are asking ourselves what interpreting and analyzing media practices – together with media texts themselves – can tell us about contemporary society. The first step in theory construction: being aware that we are interpretative beings. Always. As researchers, it is important to know that we start building theory right from the beginning of our project. Theorizing is already happening when we begin interpreting our data. Theorizing is already happening when we start to think about the story our material tells. And, maybe most importantly, theorizing is a process. Theory is always actively constructed, Lyn and Tom Richards (1994) say, it cannot be 'found'. They quote data visualizations wizards Miles and Huberman who disabuse us of the idea that theory is like 'little lizards' under rocks. You don't turn over a rock and hey, there's theory! Theory is built on "mental maps, abstracted webs of meaning, that the analyst lays over bits of data to give them shape without doing violence to them" (Miles and Huberman 1984, 83). As researchers – and especially as media and culture researchers – it is our challenge and our responsibility to weave those webs (Richards and Richards 1994, 170). Responsibility, here, not only means to do 'justice' to our data but also to help build an understanding of society. What we collectively wish for and dream of to create a better and more livable world, what excites, scares, annoys us. The question for this chapter is how to do exactly that:

How do we go from the 'opinions' and fragmented
observations and experiences of individuals to reconstructing
shared cultural knowledge?

In other words, we are thinking about how to weave interpretive webs with respect for the data – and thereby build theory. A disclaimer: theorizing is an act of power. An act that imposes your understanding onto

DOI: 10.4324/9781003315421-10

reality. It is a claim that you know what the broader logic of social and cultural phenomena and beliefs is. An assertion that you understand what others are 'really' saying and what their words mean. Again: a huge responsibility! Although we see audiences as active everyday media makers in media and cultural analysis, twentieth-century notions of the professional as 'expert interpreter' still linger on. No wonder, it gives researchers status and authority and, quite frankly, an income. This chapter, however, invites you to try on a slightly different researcher identity.

The researcher, the theorist, the detective

When you think about what kind of researcher you want to be, we hope that the answer could sound something like this: someone attuned to how meaning changes, sometimes fast, sometimes slow. Someone who knows to beware of overfocus, and someone open to different and emerging practices and patterns. Someone who can move beyond a personal zone of frustration or discomfort to learn something new. Someone who recognizes the value in everyday conversations, and their importance in understanding what matters. Someone who uses technologies from search engines to scraper tools, from bulletin boards to online threads to track meaning-making in action. Someone who is ethically responsible and treats participants with respect and integrity, whether online or offline. Someone who does not embody knowledge and oversight but is more like a detective following the trail of meaning making. Some of these are attitudes – but most are actually practices, ways of thinking and doing research!

The previous chapters have introduced you to different methods, and how these methods are always a sequence of decisions that potentially shift and change what you can and will find. Here, we are adding a new dimension to this: making sense of your findings means putting them into a larger context: social, cultural, political, as relevant to a specific place, a specific culture, a specific platform. In doing so, research on 'old' media can help us to understand 'new' media, 'old' methods offer new insights when applied to 'new' media and analyzing 'new' media can tell us something about 'old' practices. Mere summaries or superficial accounts cannot do that, and neither can media examples by themselves. Theorization, however, can.

Context, context, context

A good starting point to make sense of everyday cross-media practices – and theorizing cross-media audiences – is the *Cultural Circuit*: how does the media industry 'feed' itself, where do news stories come from, how are ideas for content developed and pitched, how do today's professional amateurs operate? Understanding yourself as a 'detective-researcher' puts you in a position to uncover and explore the hidden links between different media. For example, how professional-amateurs – 'produsers' like social media influencers – have broken the monopoly of broadcasting systems. Or how the aesthetics of TikTok reference social blogging platforms of the 2000s. Importantly, this way of thinking is not 'exclusive' for researchers but also informs creative industry and media professionals, amateur media makers and audience members with no 'producerly' interest in media texts at all. To make sense of one media text (a film, a news item, a social video, a television show…), we think about the ones we have seen before. We put them into context.

In a research project, you have to maintain focus (or your project will never finish). But you also need to return to querying how contexts matter:

- when patterns start to emerge, for instance, it helps us to check for other contexts than the one that you have been researching. You will see that sometimes social power relations play out very differently in different countries, or on different platforms
- when working with media practices, it is tempting to remain within the media sphere. However, media texts speak to us because they connect with everyday practices, experiences and feelings in our life worlds – and tracing these connections may lead you to unexpected findings

The best part of audience research, in our opinion, is exactly this detective work. Focusing and refocusing, checking back and forth. Diving deep into a conversation, to emerge and zoom out for the larger picture. Or, in detective terms: collecting evidence, putting it under the microscope, tracing these residues to collect more evidence…

Research example: the many sides of (discussing) *Bridgerton*

What if the evidence could possibly point you into different directions? In the case study presented in *Chapter 9* on the Regency romance *Bridgerton* (Netflix 2020-ongoing), we were confronted with exactly this question: while we are reading the everyday criticism emerging under YouTube reaction videos as a performance of cultural citizenship (Hermes 2024), the same data could have also been used for an article about adaptations. The Netflix series is based on a best-selling book series, and often, audiences are not altogether happy with what has happened with 'their' books (Geraghty 2007). Heated discussion about questions of consent could also have been used as the starting point for an inquiry into contemporary sexual culture.

Piecing the individual strands of data – of evidence – together can sometimes happen quickly and intuitively, especially if you started out with a clear sense of which theoretical direction to take. Other times, your detective work might be slower until your research material 'clicks'. While this might be daunting at first, do not give up too quickly! To move from your data to theory, there are two directions to take: (1) focusing & funneling and (2) contextualizing. While the first direction takes you deeper into your data, the second one helps you to zoom out and look sideways. In the following two sections, we will take you through these steps.

Direction 1: focusing and funneling through lateral summarizing

Let's assume you are doing interviews for your research project: you have found participants, have set up interview appointments, conducted the interviews and transcribed your recordings.

How to (not) transcribe your interviews

What a good transcript looks like also depends on what you want to do with it afterward. In court proceedings, for example, everything is transcribed 'verbatim' – word for word, including "Ehms" and "Ahs" and pauses. For audience research, that is not necessary – we are happy with 'intelligent', which means readable, transcripts. The 'classic' way to do this is recording your interview and then listening back to the interview while typing out the answers. This helps you to become very familiar with your material – but it also takes a whole lot of time. To help make this process easier for you, there are a variety of tools: professional transcription services, transcription software and website as well as open access tools. For example, the virtual conferencing tools like Microsoft Teams and Zoom have an integrated 'live transcription' function – which works especially well for online interviews.

You are now faced with data that need to be interpreted, made sense of. You need to theorize what you have and, at some point, you will also need to be able to refind 'good quotes' to offer proof of your theory.

In methodological terms, the first step is to understand that coding is 'lateral summarizing':

1 *Open Coding*: in open coding, you break up what your interviewees say into the smallest possible bits in order to be able to recognize those elements when they return in other interviews. Even in small research projects with < 10 interviews, it is impossible to keep track of what is where by simple note-taking. You will need a system: as we have discussed in *Chapter 3*, there are multiple ways to do open coding systematically – on paper with colored highlighters, in excel, in specific software. Remain open to the possibility that segments need to have *more than one code*. Theorization, which we are moving toward here, often depends on the strange contradictions and paradoxes that lurk just beneath the surface of most conversations

2 *Clustering*: the long lists of open codes derived from transcripts or a data set, now need clustering. Ask yourself questions like: which codes actually say the same thing? What happens when you re-read the interview segments that these codes were derived from? Peeling away the layers of what people feel they should say, and what they might actually mean, allows you to formulate an initial summary of what your interviewees talk about. This, in turn, is coded again

3 *Labeling*: once clustered, you need good labels for your clusters. In many ways, those labels are the core of the theory that you have started developing. Theory here stands for an explanation of how (in our case) particular media are used and made meaningful in everyday life. Such an explanation needs to be reached in a systematic manner, be verifiably built on research material that is offered as proof, be true to the input of research participants and be transferable to similar social practices.

As you move through these steps, you are also moving through and across your material – laterally. Coding, summarizing, coding the summaries and summarizing these again is a lot of work. But work that is absolutely worth it! As 'social animals', people are invested in being understood by others – and will use as much of the cultural knowledge we have access to in order to make ourselves understood (Potter and Wetherell 1988). By paying attention to similarities as much as contradictions, coincidences and paradoxes open your research up to deeper meanings. Your inner detective, however, needs you to go beyond the surface without judging others, or taking the 'easy' way out. Rather than talking *about* people, audience research offers a way to work *with* audiences to understand cultural, social and political issues as the emerge in everyday conversations and interpretations.

Research example: the contradictions of having 'good' neighbors

Lyn Richards and Tom Richards (1994) developed a qualitative data software program called NUDIST – and offer a great example of how tricky it can be to understand the importance of contradictions in everyday conversation. Their example project is a study of neighborliness. Respondents all said that good neighbors are enormously important – and then offered a disclaimer of that statement which sounds significantly less positive. Neighbors should not be 'in your backyard' or 'in your pocket all the time'. They seemed to say that the best neighbors were always available for help but that you ideally never need (or see) them. Once the Richards started to realize that what people say may serve different purposes at the same time, they changed from solely 'coding for retrieval' to coding by identifying 'nodes'. These are bits of interviews where two very different things meet. Contradictions and ambiguities are such nodes, and they matter!

While data retrieval can rely on summary keywords or color codes (maybe with a letter and number combination to identify the interview, and a page or location number to mark its precise space), developing theory needs something different. It needs access to complexity and contradiction, that is, to nodal points. In practice, it needs segments to carry multiple codes for the different things that are being said. Experienced researchers will immediately use nodal point codes; if you are just starting out, stick with giving as many codes as you feel are needed. Richards and Richards say "much of the activity of coding for retrieval is a theorizing process" (1994, 148). In this process, you need to trust yourself and the story that begins to emerge.

Hence, the need for "methods of handling qualitative data (to) contain ways of catching and developing ideas, exploring fleeting hints, and drawing connections between them and the data from which they derived" (Richards and Richards 1994, 149). In addition to all of the above, as an audience researcher, you will also need to take into account how much we do not question in daily life and accept as given. The ideological effect of 'naturalizing' the status quo will need to be tackled as it will obscure much. The informants of the Richards, it turned out, in part, wanted to avoid talking about loneliness (women especially dared not say they would like to have more contact with their neighbours). They felt loneliness was an individual problem rather than a structural and gendered problem in contemporary societies in the Global North.

Direction 2: contextualizing and theorizing your data

Good coding has given you a good grasp of your material: you will be able to summarize it in different ways, along different axes. You will be able to compare for different identifications (whether in relation to gender, age, sexuality, ethnicity or whatever difference is relevant to your informants). Good open coding will also have raised your neck hair from time to time. Minor inconsistencies in a single interview have become contradictory logics – productive paradoxes – recurring across your material. Now it's time to validate your theory-to-be! Audience researcher Annette Hill (2007) says that ongoing interpretative 'work' by participants (and researchers) is always performative and interactive at the same time. Here, we will draw on her book *Restyling Factual TV: Audiences and News, Documentary and Reality Genres* as an example of how to theorize research materials. A bit of background: at the time of writing, 'fake news' had not yet become a worrying reality, nonfiction television was in a state of flux. At the start of the new millennium, reality television's intervention to turn the domain of news and facts into entertainment made audiences wonder whether what they were watching was true. Hill maps and invites her material to explain the world of her informants to her. In contrast Couldry, Livingstone and Markham's (2007) "public connection" study sought to evaluate the citizenship value of news in the early twenty-first century and undo the divide between consumption and democratic legitimacy. Also important but a completely different approach.

By contrasting how interviewees talked about the news, documentary and reality television, Hill shows how 'actuality' (what is happening really and currently) becomes a key factor in assessing factual television. Meanwhile, audiences also value 'performance' and have stable hierarchies across European countries, with news at the top and reality television at the bottom of a 'truth scale' (2007, 143). The use of the term 'actuality' is productive for theorizing her (wide-ranging) research material but also helps to stay away from 'realism'. As an ambiguous term, realism "can mean something can be real, it can appear realistic, and it can also feel familiar to us" (Hill 2007, 113). Hill's theorization opens up to understanding that 'reality' does not have a fixed set of markers – it always needs negotiation. Theory, here, in addition helps to apply insights from one part of the media world of research participants to another. For example, it becomes clear how the wish for politicians to be more 'authentic' (likely impossible for them to achieve) is linked to the shift in the media landscape with the entrance of reality television in the 1990s. In turn, the 'birth' of reality television can be traced back to the ongoing push for emancipation of minority and underrepresented groups (in this case the rather large group of 'ordinary people') and technological innovation – i.e., cameras becoming capable of high-definition videorecording, with video much and much easier and faster to mix and manipulate than film (Caldwell 1995).

Recurring metaphors and tropes in the material point Hill to how audiences invest their definitions of reality and realness with references to nature and, hence, to the opposition of natural and unnatural. When they wish for politicians to be more authentic, it is a wish for them to be more 'natural', that is: true to life. "Nature as a metaphor for the real thus becomes a touchstone, a guide to the labyrinthine world of fact and fiction, something to hold onto in the highly stylized representations of reality that dominate factual television", Hill argues. Audiences want to trust the news, but they also know that news is a representation of reality and therefore cannot be totally trusted. The following comment explains the difficult position of being a news viewer:

I kind of believe what I see when I watch the news. But I sometimes think it's also being picked. You know, like, what's important and what's not important. And you never know, you know, it can be subjective in that way. They show certain bits of a war, for example, and you don't know really what's going on with both sides. Cos they might show more of that side or. . . . And you kind of think "oh yes, yes, yes", you believe what you see. But you don't know whether you get all of it, like, a full range (30-year-old British female multimedia developer).

(Fragment from Annette Hill 2007, 135)

Hill validates her theory of the everyday 'truth' value of news in two ways: for one, she offers a great many direct quotes from interview material. In addition, her outcomes have been checked in a large survey. Her theorization hinges on the difference between *actuality* (you will recognise how 'actual' is used in and for serious news and current affairs programmes) and *performativity* (whether politicians, reality television participants, persons and presenters come across as 'believable'). In most cases, Hill's double-validation strategy will not be possible for you in a smaller research project. But: thinking about transferability definitely is! In practice, your process of theorization could involve checking for differences made by your participants between different genres, different media or different platforms. Offering quotes throughout your paper, thesis or report will also help to ground your theorization in the data – and make it all the more convincing.

Research example: reading women's magazines

In a project about reading women's magazines, interviewees told
Joke Hermes (1995) that the magazines they read were really not
that important to them. They read them at moments when they
had to wait, in 'empty time'. This might sound similar to how we
talk about scrolling on our phones today. Hermes' interviewees
repeatedly said that women's magazines offered practical information from recipes to holiday tips. Again, similar to what you find
on social media platforms like Instagram. Together, in a lateral
summary, these remarks suggest that women's magazines to their
readers were a mundane medium, nothing special – but kind of
useful. When an interviewee told Joke Hermes that she kept all the
recipes previously cut out of the magazines in plastic bags in the attic, however, this 'usefulness' became a bit questionable. It just felt
good to keep them there, was the interviewee's response. Going
back to earlier interviews and asking follow-up questions in later
ones, it became clear that all the saving of recipes and cleaning tips
but also the reading of relationship advice and dating tips were
hardly related to actual practical action. They served the rather different goal of imagining perfect selves. Using the recipes, it turned
out in other interviews, had often not led to great results. To imagine yourself a great cook, though, or the kind of friend who is able
to give someone else good advice at times of emotional upheaval
were highly valued pleasures for these readers (Hermes 1995).

How to: lean into contradictions

The contradictions in the women's magazine material came in two layers. In the first one, women's magazines were simply denied all value.
"Easily put down" is how readers characterized them. The interviewees
either didn't know why they read them or emphasized that they mostly
didn't pay proper attention to them – women's magazines were meant
to fill the time. While waiting for family members, while waiting for
patients or their own appointments, while watching not-too-gripping
television. However, readers did have preferences for specific titles and
rubrics within those magazines. This contradiction seemed to be an ideological one. A matter of taste, in a way: only a minority of informants
said they actually liked the magazines they read (mostly by using the
'guilty pleasure' metaphor introduced in *Chapter 2*). The second layer of
paradoxicality was that interviewees shifted from emphasizing the lack
of value to the fully opposite claim that women's magazines were so

useful. This, too, served an ideological goal: it justified spending money on them. More interestingly, it veiled the pleasure in imagining a perfect self. Women's magazines are useful, it turns out, but for a temporary fantasy construction.

How to: *theorize instead of assume*

Assuming that women's magazines have an effect on readers would have worked against understanding how they are meaningful. If readers of women's magazines turn out to cherish fantasies of perfect selves, is that not proof that they are influenced by women's magazines? The literature about women's magazines has long assumed this. An example is Marjorie Ferguson's book (1983) in which the editors-in-chief of women's magazines are the high priestesses of that cult. Ferguson, however, takes women's magazines to only promote heteronormativity for women. It is all about: to have and hold your man. The interviews with readers in Joke Hermes' *Reading Women's Magazines* were held at the end of the same decade Ferguson wrote in. Hermes' interviews do not point to readers being obsessed with their status as sexualized objects in a relationship with a man. On the contrary, their fantasies about better versions of themselves hinge on being able to know and do things. To be a great cook, to know what advice to give someone whose child has died. In addition, when validating the theory that women's magazines offer the gratification of moments of reimagining oneself, it was also clear that readers were well aware that these were moments of fantasy which they relished nonetheless. Thinking in terms of 'effect' would have made it difficult not to see readers as victims and to follow their convoluted route to reading pleasure.

How to: *follow up on existing research*

As we have pointed out at the beginning of this section, the ways women's magazines were understood in the 1990s feel weirdly familiar to how social media frequently comes up in everyday conversation. Do you save Instagram videos the same way that Hermes' interviewees saved magazine articles – only in the 'cloud' as the modern attic? Three decades later, it might be worthwhile to ask audiences about how they use Instagram, TikTok and other social media platforms. Likely, there is an interesting story there as well. A first layer will doubtlessly again be organized to counter further inquiry, as an ideological barrier. It might be: I am so addicted, or I really don't care. But what comes after that? Is it checking codes and norms (and an exercise in governmentality), is it inspiration or dreaming and part of entrepreneurial selfhood, as Sarah

Banet-Weiser (2017) has suggested in her research on girl culture? It will pay to *not* assume that it will only be young women watching videos on how to look perfect – and to realize that the great make-up tutorials of the mid-2010s were made by trans women and drag superstars. Think beyond the lateral summary to nodal points. Contextualize broadly and step outside of your own lifeworld experience. Embrace the weird, the funny and the discomfort. It will be worth your while.

Practice exercise: going back to the 'source'

Throughout this book, we have emphasized how meaning-making happens in and through everyday conversations – and having an everyday conversation about your research can do exactly this. Collecting, analyzing and theorizing your data are often connected to your intuition, to following hunches activated by references in the material. Based on one of your own projects, we now want to challenge you to go back to your participants and ask them to comment on your outcomes. Does this feel 'true' to them? Do they recognize the patterns you are seeing? Is there something missing from them? Can they explain where and why they disagree with your interpretation? Include what you realize in this conversation in your report!

References

Banet-Weiser, Sarah. 2017. "'I'm Beautiful the Way I Am': Empowerment, Beauty, and Aesthetic Labour." In *Aesthetic Labour*, edited by Ana Sofia Elias, Rosalind Gill, and Christina Scharff, 265–82. London: Palgrave Macmillan UK. https://doi.org/10.1057/978-1-137-47765-1_15.

Caldwell, John Thornton. 1995. *Televisuality: Style, Crisis, and Authority in American Television*. Communication, Media, and Culture. New Brunswick, NJ: Rutgers University Press.

Couldry, Nick, Sonia M. Livingstone, and Tim Markham. 2007. *Media Consumption and Public Engagement: Beyond the Presumption of Attention*. Consumption and Public Life. Basingstoke, Hampshire ; New York: Palgrave Macmillan.

Ferguson, Marjorie. 1983. *Forever Feminine: Women's Magazines and the Cult of Femininity*. London/Exeter (NH): Heinemann.

Geraghty, Christine. 2007. *Now a Major Motion Picture: Film Adaptations of Literature and Drama*. Genre and Beyond. Lanham: Rowman & Littlefield Publishers.

Hermes, Joke. 1995. *Reading Women's Magazines: An Analysis of Everyday Media Use*. Cambridge: Polity Press.

———. 2024. *Cultural Citizenship and Popular Culture. The Art of Listening*. London: Routledge.

Hill, Annette. 2007. *Restyling Factual TV: Audiences and News, Documentary and Reality Genres*. London/New York: Routledge.

Miles, Matthew B., and A. M. Huberman. 1984. *Qualitative Data Analysis: A Sourcebook of New Methods*. Beverly Hills: Sage Publications.

Potter, John, and Margaret Wetherell. 1988. "Discourse Analysis and the Identification of Interpretative Repertoires." In *Analysing Everyday Explanation: A Casebook of Methods*, 168–83. London: Sage Publications.

Richards, Lyn, and Tom Richards. 1994. "From Filing Cabinet to Computer." In *Analyzing Qualitative Data*, edited by Alan Bryman and Bob Burgess, 146–72. London: Routledge. https://doi.org/10.4324/9780203413081.

Part III

Case studies

Methods in action

8   Discourse analysis in practice

Private attraction, public (dis)approval? Negotiating what to make of Netflix's *You*

Method: single case study of tweets about a popular TV series

Single case studies do not allow generalization about audiences, nor about platforms. What they can do is help reconstruct the logic in how, on a specific platform, a series is made sense of. A case can be made for the wider relevance (or 'transferability') of the findings by checking discussion on other platforms, or by other means (such as a small open-question survey in Facebook groups the researcher is a member of). More commonly, insights gained on a particular body of data are used to theorize findings, that is to bring findings to a higher level of understanding (see Chapter 7). Rather than summarize Twitter comments, theorizing allows access to a new story (or stories) that help understand cultural codes, customs and implicit understandings.

Research question

The research question for this kind of research is an open question, often starting from 'how'? How is the series You made sense of on Twitter? Open questions can focus on specific themes: what pleasure does the Netflix series You affords viewers going by comments on Twitter?

Data collection

Collecting data on social platforms has become more difficult after 2018 when the privacy of individuals became better protected. Here, we followed relevant hashtags until no new tweets were found.

DOI: 10.4324/9781003315421-12

Data analysis

The tweets were sorted for their focus, their key arguments and their rhetorical style. This delivered a broadly thematic analysis, which when going through the material, morphed into three frames. Another option is to reconstruct 'interpretative repertoires' or pay close attention to style and focus, e.g., on how Twitter can be used as a coping mechanism, a fail-safe space. You makes for an exceptional example for two reasons. For one, the series does not offer a single, clear frame of reference. Those watching the series had to wonder why they kept watching. This entails finding arguments that challenge each other – it shows how we often employ very different (and contradictory) frames when making sense of media texts. The goal is to map these frames and see what they have to tell us about how viewers, including ourselves, experience the world and their lives today.

Key concepts

Frame in this chapter refers to a rhetorical means of defining an issue or a question in such a way that specific interpretations are encouraged and others discouraged. The term is often used in communication science in relation to political news (together with 'priming'). Key theorists of frames and framing are Erving Goffman (1974) and Robert Entman (1993).

Identification is a tricky concept. It invites a psychological research mind-set which has the drawback of focusing on individuals and psychopathology. Identification, however, can also be used for media and cultural studies. Jason Mittell (2015) breaks down 'identification' into useful aspects such as attunement and allegiance in his book Complex TV, *making it a useful tool for qualitative audience research.*

Star text: media entertainment is a multilayered practice. As audiences, we knit together different kinds of knowledge, judgments and emotions. Richard Dyer (1998) suggests we 'read' bodies as if they are texts. An actor's earlier roles and looks thus become part of how we make sense of them as a character, for instance in a TV series.

Hannibal Lecter, Dexter Morgan, Joe Goldberg: all lead characters in television entertainment – and all serial killers. The three of them raise the question whether there are fictional characters so monstrous that it is hard to imagine anyone would want to consider themselves their fan. But that is exactly what we do. This chapter focuses on a single case study with an open question: how is it possible to like the manipulative, stalking, serial-killing lead character in the Netflix hit series *You*? It is written from a 'we' perspective. Not to avoid using 'I' or to assume that our readers will automatically share our perspective but to foreground that we are challenging our own discomfort. We too are intrigued by this show and do not want to hide behind an authoritative voice that makes it easy to stand in judgment of other viewers. Writing from a 'we' perspective makes us 'accessories', co-conspirators in turning Joe Goldberg's really unacceptable behavior into – well into what exactly? An attractive man wrapping violent actions in romantic gestures apparently can horrify and fascinate at the same time.

More formally, the question for audience research is: what interpretative strategies do viewers employ to make sense of Netflix' hit series *You*? As viewer-researchers, we have an inkling that *You*'s genre-bending mode of storytelling is important in allowing the seemingly impossible feat of presenting a lovable jealous murderer. This chapter offers an example of how to take on board insights gained by using the tools of textual analysis while centering and respecting how audiences 'read' the series.

Single case study versus multiple case study research: value, validity, testing and building theory

Apart from questions of morality and of women's complicity in toxic masculinity that immediately spring to mind when thinking of *You* – there are methodological questions to be considered. For instance: why do a single case study? An alternative approach would be to do a comparative analysis in a 'multiple case study design' (Yin 2017). Comparing cases has the advantage of giving a study higher validity. It offers the reader more means to check the claims of the researchers. In comparing, emerging ideas can be tested, which is where theorization begins. In this chapter, we use an analysis of *You*'s storytelling to contextualize discussion on Twitter. Rather than focus on individuals, we look for shared sentiments and key arguments across tweets. That way we are able to chart the cultural logic viewers refer to when making sense of *You*. In turn, this allows for reflection on gendered attraction and sexuality against the background of (online) dating in the twenty-first century.

According to Cornel Sandvoss fandom is a "space used by fans for the articulation and reflection of self" (2003, 27). Controversial, yet beloved characters – yes, even serial killers – can help us figure out who we are. Although the serial killer has been an object of the (sub)genre of the police procedural for decades, the past years have seen a much larger number of 'anti-heroes' than before. Remarkably, the serial killer has morphed from antagonist to protagonist. *Hannibal* (NBC) and *Dexter* (Showtime), for instance, are given a more or less reasonable explanation for their transgressions – psychological childhood trauma and an over-sized sense of morality, respectively. As these shows follow the logic of the crime procedural, we find ourselves in recognizable tales. Academics such as Stephanie Green note that each episodes

> anticipates and delivers a spectacular kill scene, each catches a murderer, solves a mystery, relieves the audience, and momentarily restores the social order – albeit a trifle bloodstained – providing viewers with that tidy feeling of having wiped down the benches and taken out the trash.
> (2012, 583)

You is notably different: here, we are introduced to a killer protagonist who takes us way further across the boundary of morality.

You, Netflix and the Zeitgeist

Based on Caroline Kepnes' novel *You*, the television series launched on the American network Lifetime in September 2018, but was "propelled into the cultural zeitgeist" (Stern 2020) through the international launch on the streaming platform Netflix in December of the same year. According to data provided by Netflix, the show was an instant success with close to 40 million viewers for the first season within the first month of streaming (Kafka 2019). Although these numbers are not independently confirmed, the series has been the topic of conversation in traditional media outlets – with reviews, articles and interviews from the *New York Times* to *Fox News* – and on social media. This points to the significance of the series as a "global cultural phenomenon" (Larson 2019). One year after the release of the first season, the second season aired exclusively on Netflix in the popular 'binge-watchable' format. According to Netflix, the second season of the series ranks as the fifth most popular series on the streaming platform in 2019 (Andreeva 2019). As it was launched late December, that is an especially impressive achievement.

The official description on Netflix reads: "A dangerously charming, intensely obsessive young man goes to extreme measures to insert himself into the lives of those he is transfixed by". Joe, the charming young man, is played by former *Gossip Girl* heartthrob Penn Badgley. The objects of obsession of this "charming creeper extraordinaire" (Di Trolio 2019), "deranged stalker" (Larson 2019) and "handsome-but-deadly protagonist" (Ferguson 2019) are Guinevere Beck and Love Quinn in the first and second season respectively. The descriptions – 'charming creeper', 'handsome-but-deadly' – highlight the juxtaposition between the character's charm and attractiveness and his monstrous actions. In both seasons, his 'inserting himself into the lives of those he is transfixed by' involves online and offline stalking and escalating violence. He ultimately murders Guinevere Beck in a bookstore-basement-turned-plexiglass-prison at the end of the first season. How can a character, who stalks a woman, kidnaps and murders his presumed competition (both male and female) and ultimately kills his beloved, qualify as a romantic lead and become an object of fan love?

Contrary to *Hannibal* or *Dexter*, *You* does not offer a redeeming narrative for Joe Goldberg. The romanticization of psychological abuse is applauded by some for "igniting conversations around hot-button topics like abuse, social media safety, and white male privilege" (Stern 2020). Clearly, "the persuasive force of images depends not only on the images themselves, but also on the frame we use to interpret them" (Smith 2017, 166). So what frame or frames apply here? We found three: *Experience, Real Fiction* and *Humour and Disbelief*. The makers seem to have opted for polarizing the audience by portraying a series' protagonist who is open to competing interpretations. While attraction to an (apparent) villain is not new – considering *Dexter*'s Dexter Morgan or *Buffy the Vampire Slayer*'s Spike – *You* fueled impressively passionate discussion among critics and viewers. To track what frames are used, we focus on tweets published at the end of 2019 (just after the release of the second season). On Twitter, viewers unburden their hearts:

> *Said this already but @PennBadgley is breaking my heart once again as Joe. What is it about him?* ♡

With 1.462 Favs, 97 retweets and a large number of comments including one from Penn Badgley himself, this very tweet is emblematic of online viewer engagement with the show, the actor and each other. The tweet and Penn Badgley's response – "A: He is a murderer" (Badgley 2019) emphasize the intended double meaning of the series. To critics Joe Goldberg is a "problematic and disconcerting" character (Zaragoza 2020) but what did viewers make of Joe? What interpretative strategies did they employ to explain, frame and validate their love for the series and its main protagonist? Twitter and YouTube are easy-to-access platforms for taking a closer look at viewer practices. Twitter is organized around open, visible and searchable hashtags, contrary to (for example) closed Facebook groups. Using an open-source archiving tool, tweets speaking to viewers' paradoxical attraction to Joe Goldberg were collected, after the release of the second season, between December 2019 and April 2020.

Tweets in English using the hashtag #NetflixYou, #YouNetflix, #YouSeason1, #YouSeason2 or the names of the main characters #JoeGoldberg, #GuinevereBeck and #LoveQuinn were collected and analyzed. After an initial search query, the hashtag #You was excluded from the analysis, and it was not specific enough to find material about the series. In addition to open-source tools, commercial tools such as Coosto also offer trial subscriptions. To collect data for a class assignment, you can also check with your university about existing subscriptions.

Frame I: "But I feel for him, ya know?" Private attraction as shared experience

Joe Goldberg is – objectively – bad. He is not a vigilante anti-hero who punishes bad persons. No, Joe Goldberg's aggression is directed at those who have personally wronged him or whom he claims to love. Without a redeeming storyline or motivation behind the character's actions, viewers need to interrogate their private attraction. Why would you feel attracted to this guy? The *Experience* frame is built on tweets in which viewers ask others whether they recognize this:

Watching @YouNetflix and wondering why I'm attracted to this freaking maniac! Tell me I'm not the only one?! Gotta love a bad guy #YouNetflix

So am I the only psycho who actually likes Joe from #netflixYOU

Does anyone else find joe/will attractive or do I just need help? #YouNetflix

The tweets show a balancing act. They acknowledge the tweeter's questionable attraction to Joe (am I the only psycho; do I need help) *and* suggest that this is not abnormal but a condition others will also experience. *You* – as a text – explicitly invites identification with its main character. A 'light' form of textual analysis is useful to contextualize this conundrum. From the perspective of narrative analysis, You is interesting for not only telling its story from the perspective of Joe Goldberg but for overlaying the visual narrative with his voice-over. This produces 'identification' with Joe and increases your need as a viewer (speaking as viewers ourselves) to discuss the series with others. Potentially useful is E. Ann Kaplan insight that television adds an emotional dimension to processes of identification. "Along with desiring identity via identifying, we also desire emotional connectedness. Identity is constructed in the process of establishing emotional connection. We respond to being 'hailed' because the process of subject-formation offers both identity and emotional connectedness" (1989, 197). If television is about becoming a subject, of achieving personhood within a particular understanding of the world, then it is not so strange to ask for a confirmation of 'not being the only one'. It is certainly more than a deflection of moral judgment for identifying with an immoral main character.

You may wonder whether viewers identify with Joe or whether they fancy him? The answer is that they do both when using the *Experience* frame. Joe can only be attractive when you step into *You*'s storyworld and accept its invitation to suspend moral judgment. The comments make clear that suspension of moral judgment is quite a price to pay. In confessing to their attraction to Joe, viewers take their 'private' admiration for a serial killer 'public'. In establishing that this is a *shared* experience, viewers absolve one another.

Don't we all need a Joe #YouNetflix

I'm falling in love with Joe! Send help!

My boy is not bad he just does not meet the right people

Joe is such a psychopath, but I feel for him, ya know? #YouNetflix

Ik something was wrong with me when I agreed to everything Joe did 🔪🍝 *#JoeGoldberg #YouNetflix*

The *Experience* frame manages a paradox. By suggesting that you may not be the only one to feel attracted to Joe, a private feeling and lack of moral outrage become a semipublic, group phenomenon. Instead of having to deflect judgment, viewers connect through Joe. They repeat similar sentiments in separate comments and like, retweet and comment on the tweets of others. A sense of community is built. A group confession is hardly a confession at all.

Frame II: "I swear I was #beck in a psychotic relationship" Connecting TV fiction and lived reality

While the #You tweets seek and build shared experience through televisual viewing, there is also a running theme that connects the narrative of *You* to personal experience as part of contemporary societal and cultural realities. Nell suggests that "the delight of the narrative is its safety: the story-world, unlike dream worlds and the real world, is above all safe and nonthreatening" (Nell 2002, 17). Comments within this frame challenge this distinction. Connecting characters and their actions to their own lived reality does not feel 'safe'. Rather, the narrative offers 'emotional realism' as Ien Ang (1985) called it. In an experimental communication study, Alice Hall found that "personal experience not only served as evidence" but that for viewers "it established a standard to which specific media portrayals were compared" (2003, 631).

> *Omg I'm just now watching #YouNetflix & I swear I was #beck in a psychotic relationship*
>
> *i dated joe from You for almost a year and i don't know how i didnt end up like beck* 😳 *#YouNetflix*
>
> *So today I saw the guy that used to stalk me 24/7 in high school and my anxiety said* ☑☑☑ *#JoeGoldberg*
>
> *When you keep falling for toxic boys #joegoldberg*
>
> *Got some stalkers don't know if I should be scared or flattered #joegoldberg?*

With exclamations like 'I swear I was #beck in a psychotic relationship' and 'I don't know how I didn't end up like beck', the comments drawing on the *Real Fiction* frame connect personal experiences and the television narrative. The series offers the possibility to share difficult experiences and emotions with others. In this frame, as in the first frame, the boundary dissolves between the portrayal of a fictional relationship and real experiences in the lives of the viewers. Interestingly, this second frame extends beyond being a victim. It is also used to emphasize identifying with the main character of the series:

> *I suck at dating cause once i like you.. i turn in to Joe nfs* 😭😭 *#YouNetflix*
>
> *Not to be dramatic but being ignored reallllllllllyyyy triggers my inner Joe Goldberg #YouNetflix #YouSeasonTwo*
>
> *Being ignored really triggers the Joe in me.* 😕😵 *#YouNetflix*
>
> *You know Joe from 'YOU' on Netflix. I be like that sometimes. #you #netfilx #netflixyou*

Although the tweets (implicitly) acknowledge that Joe's behavior is unacceptable, the frame normalizes questionable dating practices. The *You* comments are a gateway to talk about dating, toxic masculinity and how to understand privacy and intimacy at a time in which everyone and everything is 'public' in the online world. However fictional, what happens on the screen feels real(istic) to these viewers. It corresponds "to the way (they) currently perceive the world" (Fiske and Hartley 1978, 128). *You* clearly is eminently plausible:

> *The #creepy thing is that this guy actually exists in real life. Makes people rethink their #socialmedia sharing! #YouNetflix #JoeGoldberg #stalker*
>
> *Its funny how Joe tries to pretend like hes happier in a better place w the safer, less problematic Karen but still longs for (and attempts to deny it) the skanky, slightly dishonest, troublesome Beck. How many times have we (including myself) done this in our lives? #YouNetflix*
>
> *Is there a penalty for lying and manipulating to break someone's heart? I guess I suck at choosing the good guys, but I'm good at spotting the bad guys. #YouNetflix*

In the tweets, note repeated references to 'guys out there' and 'good boys' vs. 'bad boys'. It hints, or so it seems, at shared experiences of toxic masculinity. By romanticizing his actions and accepting his self-understanding as one of the 'good guys', Joe Goldberg apparently can be seen as the opposite of toxic masculinity. According to television critic Roisin Lanigan: "He projects the persona of the anti-fuckboi" (2019). In an exemplary scene from the first season, Joe muses "Sometimes I swear I'm the only real feminist you know". His is not a masculinity, he thinks, "that glorifies stoicism, strength, virility, and dominance,

---

Penn Badgley and the 'star text'

Where does the actor end and the role begin? In the love and hate for television characters boundaries between the fictional and the real are not always clear. Film scholar Richard Dyer suggests we understand the star-as-text, a composite construction. In *You*, the actor and the character have merged to the extent that their names, Penn Badgley and Joe Goldberg, are used interchangeably, The reference to what is ultimately the same 'body' becomes even more complicated with the inclusion of Badgley's earlier roles. His breakout role Dan Humphrey shaped his public image – and potentially how viewers see him as Joe Goldberg. This is what Dyer means when he says that "the star is effective in the construction of character" (1998, 126). Between being the romantic lead in *Gossip Girl* and the paranoid psycho-feminist in *You*, Badgley has mostly focused on a music career – and not offered as more reference frames.

and that is socially maladaptive or harmful to mental health" ("Toxic Masculinity", 2020). Really, Joe?

Beyond linking to past experience, the *Real Fiction* frame is used as a warning. Comments echo the sentiment that dating and relationships are fraught with danger in the twenty-first century. In the last episode of season 1, Guinevere Beck writes about her relationship with Joe – and her relationships with men in general. At that point, she is locked in a bookstore-basement-turned-plexiglass-prison. She addresses herself, but also the viewers through second person address, when she concludes: "You learned you didn't have whatever magic turned a beast into a prince [...] Now in his castle you understand: Prince Charming and Bluebeard are the same man". Beck's soliloquy suggests that *You* is a cautionary tale. That fairytale fantasies and real-world experiences are very different, is a scary thing to realize.

> *2 days ago I was living my best life, carefree, a lol stress about school and shit. Today, after 15 episodes of #YouNetflix i'm becoming so paranoid and seeing everybody from joe's perspective HELP LMAO*

> *Watching #YouNetflix starting to get trust issues...*

> *Does anyone else keep seeing Self Storage places differently since watching #YouNetflix series 2? Every time I pass one I wonder who's being held hostage inside*

The *Real Fiction* frame points forward to a third frame through which to deal with the tension between fictional events and real experiences: humor.

Frame III "I REAL LIVE said 'what in the Joe?'" Sharing humor and disbelief

It is the logic of social media to try to increase the reach of one's comments, and humor is an important tool to do so (Highfield 2015). Humorous tweets certainly gained a larger group of discussants for *You*: They bring a third frame into being, offering another type of connection and shared value creation.

> *Hats are the best. Bad hair day? Put on a hat. Sun in your eyes? Wear a hat. Need a disguise to stalk your girlfriend after you just killed her best friend? Put on a hat #joegoldberg*

> *Day 1764 of Being Single: I'm reconsidering my method of approach. Might try the 'Joe Goldberg' method😬 #YouNetflix*

> *This dude just asked me for my address. I REAL LIVE said "what in the Joe?" 😂😂😂 #YouNetflix*

Joe Goldberg be texting back and making phone calls while killing people. Don't settle for less ladies. If he loves you he will text you back. Lol #YouNetflix #you #PennBadgley

Humorous exaggerations attach to the same content and possibly the same feelings and emotions that the first two frames do. Instead of connecting with others over falling for the 'wrong' guy, the *Humour and Disbelief* frame consoles and relativizes. It tempers *You's*frightening portrait of contemporary romance. Expressions like: 'Don't settle for less ladies' and 'Might try the Joe Goldberg method', at face value, appear disarming. These funny and eminently retweetable comments, however, also function as another way of sharing the experience of watching – and loving – Joe and *You*. After all, these comments are only funny to those who can relate – through their pop cultural knowledge of the series but also through understanding the real-life experiences the series reflects on.

Beyond humorous exaggeration as a strategy to deflect and disarm the scary and not entirely unlikely message of the series, there is also disbelief in these tweets. Discrepancy between personal experiences and the narrative portrayed in a series as well as discrepancies with established televisual conventions make it impossible for emotional and other forms of realism to be established. Here, we return to narrative consistency in the sense of "realistic programming that is internally coherent, that doesn't contradict itself, and leaves nothing jarringly unexplained" (Hall 2003, 636). Even in the considerable latitude afforded to fictional narratives, what happens next – or what doesn't happen – in *You* is experienced as disruption, as simply unrealistic.

How does nobody notice Joe? *#YouNetflix*

Just started watching #YouNetflix Why are her windows wide open all the time? The lights inside are too bright. If you're a New Yorker, you're smarter than this -_-

So #YouNetflix is basically a clumsy #Dexter that just gets somehow lucky with all the things he do along the way.

😵

A 'clumsy Dexter' getting away with his crimes and the naive behavior of the other characters – 'If you're a New Yorker, you're smarter than this' – also spawn disbelief. Instead of leading back to lived reality, *You* disappoints. Comments within this frame emphasize the discrepancies between the tweeter's own experiences – often presented as standing in for the experience of others as well – and the narrative. *You*'s evasion of a clear genre definition here returns to haunt it. "The progress of detective fiction in general is one that goes from order disrupted to order re-established" (Santaulària 2007, 55). *You* deviates from this logic. Extreme tweets explicitly demand that order be re-established:

> *Pls tell me there's going to be some justice and he ends up in prison. We have enough white guys getting away with stuff in reality*
>
> *Season three of 'You' should just be the Criminal Minds team trying to solve all of Joes murders #Netflix #YouNetflix*
>
> *Honestly Joe Goldberg constantly fucks up he deserves to get caught, send Dexter in to show him how it's really done #you #joegoldberg #dexter*
>
> *Ever wonder what #joegoldberg would look like on #dexters table?*

Calling for justice, perhaps enacted through other fictional characters such as *Dexter*'s serial killing main character Dexter Morgan or the forensic specialists of *Criminal Minds* is funny. At the same time, it functions handily as a deflection of judgment for potentially liking the series 'too much'.

Conclusion

In their work on fandom, Brianna Dym and Casey Fiesler have argued that "there is a creeping sense among fans that private and public spaces online might be collapsing into one another" (2018). Casual viewers too might experience this. It would explain how public online spaces like Twitter and YouTube (and others) allow for interaction among virtual strangers. With a focus on words like 'we' and 'you know' and direct address, the tweets seek (public) approval (or ask to 'send help'). They are a form of 'watercooler talk'. This case study shows how viewers navigate their experience of watching *You* on Twitter through three frames, *Experience*, *Real Fiction* and *Humour and Disbelief*. The frames help to come to terms with loving 'hateable' guys – and perhaps even with a sense that all likable guys might turn out to be creeps. Interestingly, tweets also point to identifying with Joe and vicariously enjoying the character's invisible power over others. Tweeting is like confessing. Retweets and comments absolve one of one's crimes. Other tweets ridicule the series or dismiss it for not offering a form of realism viewers can inhabit.

Combining a thematic analysis (that led us to the frames) with insights from narratology and television studies shows how a single case study can be persuasive and a valid method. It also allowed us to show how textual analysis can help make sense of audience materials without taking away from the very real emotional, intellectual and affective investments of viewers. As it seems, audiences are not going to stop watching soon: in February 2023, Netflix released the fourth season for its hit show *You* – with a fifth one already confirmed. It seems we all need a #Joe in our lives, right?

References

Ang, Ien, Della Couling, and Ien Ang. 1985. *Watching Dallas: Soap Opera and the Melodramatic Imagination*. London: Routledge.

Andreeva, Nellie. 2019. "'Murder Mystery', 'Stranger Things' Lead Netflix's List Of Most Popular Movies, TV Series & Specials Of 2019." Deadline (blog). December 30, 2019. https://deadline.com/2019/12/murder-mystery-stranger-things-3-netflix-list-of-most-popular-movies-tv-series-of-2019-the-witcher-you-netflix-what-we-watched-2019-1202818337/.

Badgley, Penn. 2019. "(3) Penn Badgley on Twitter: 'A: He Is a Murderer https://T. Co/G2g4f3JvaF' / Twitter." Twitter. September 1, 2019. https://twitter.com/pennbadgley/status/1083088038216024066.

Di Trolio, Alex. n.d. *Penn Badgley on His New Show "You."* Accessed February 3, 2020. https://soundcloud.com/alexditrolio/penn-badgley-on-his-new-show-you.

Dyer, Richard. 1998. *Stars*. New ed. London: BFI Pub.

Dym, Brianna, and Casey Fiesler. 2018. "Generations, Migrations, and the Future of Fandom's Private Spaces." *Transformative Works and Cultures* 28. https://doaj.org/article/29130a2da9fd44979df53a7db01689bf.

Entman, Robert M. 1993. "Framing: Toward Clarification of a Fractured Paradigm." *JournalofCommunication* 43(4): 51–58. https://doi.org/10.1111/j.1460-2466.1993.tb01304.x.

Ferguson, LaToya. 2019. "'You' Season 2 Is a Dangerously Compelling and Worthy Follow-Up | IndieWire." December 24, 2019. https://www.indiewire.com/2019/12/netflix-you-season-2-review-1202199214/.

Fiske, John, and John Hartley. 1978. *Reading Television*. 2nd ed. Hoboken: Taylor and Francis.

Goffman, Erving. 1986. *Frame Analysis: An Essay on the Organization of Experience*. Northeastern University Press ed. Boston, MA: Northeastern University Press.

Green, Stephanie. 2012. "Desiring Dexter : The Pangs and Pleasures of Serial Killer Body Technique." *Continuum: Journal of Media & Cultural Studies* 26 (4): 579–88. https://doi.org/10.1080/10304312.2012.698037.

Hall, Alice. 2003. "Reading Realism: Audiences' Evaluations of the Reality of Media Texts." *Journal of Communication* 53 (4): 624–41. https://doi.org/10.1111/j.1460-2466.2003.tb02914.x.

Highfield, Tim. 2015. "Tweeted Joke Life Spans and Appropriated Punch Lines: Practices Around Topical Humor on Social Media." *International Journal of Communication (19328036)* 9 (January): 2713–34.

Kafka, Peter. 2019. "Netflix Is Finally Sharing (Some of) Its Audience Numbers for Its TV Shows and Movies. Some of Them Are Huge." Vox. January 17, 2019. https://www.vox.com/2019/1/17/18187234/netflix-views-numbers-first-time-bird-box-bodyguard-you-sex-education.

Kaplan, E. Ann. 1989. "E. Ann Kaplan." *Camera Obscura: Feminism, Culture, and Media Studies* 7 (2–3 (20–21)): 194–99. https://doi.org/10.1215/02705346-7-2-3_20-21-194.

Larson, Lauren. 2019. "Penn Badgley on How He Lived Long Enough to Become the Villain | GQ." GQ. Accessed February 4, 2020. https://www.gq.com/story/penn-badgley-lived-long-enough-to-become-the-villain.

Lanigan, Roisin. 2019. "Netflix's 'You' Shows the Problem We Still Have Separating Romance from Emotional Abuse." *I-D* (blog). January 4, 2019. https://i-d.vice.com/en_us/article/qvqqjv/netflixs-you-series-1-ending-explained-emotional-abuse-stalking.

Mittell, Jason. 2015. Complex TV: The Poetics of Contemporary Television Storytelling. New York: New York University Press.

Nell, Victor. 2002. "Mythic Structures in Narrative." In *Narrative Impact: Social and Cognitive Foundations*, edited by Melanie C. Green, Jeffrey J. Strange, and Timothy C. Brock, 17–38. Taylor & Francis.

Sandvoss, Cornel. 2003. *A Game of Two Halves Football, Television, and Globalization. Comedia.* London: Routledge.

Santaulària, Isabel. 2007. "'The Great Good Place' No More? Integrating and Dismantling Oppositional Discourse in Some Recent Examples of Serial Killer Fiction." *Atlantis, Revista de La Asociación Española de Estudios Anglo-Norteamericanos* 29 (1): 55–67.

Smith, Greg. 2017. "Realism." In *Keywords for Media Studies*, edited by Laurie Ouellette and Jonathan Gray, 166–168 NYU Press.

Stern, Claire. 2020. "Penn Badgley on You, Date Nights with Domino Kirke, and the 2020 Election." InStyle. January 14, 2020. https://www.instyle.com/celebrity/penn-badgley-you-interview-social-media-creep.

Yin, Robert K. 2017. *Case Study Research and Applications: Design and Methods.* Los Angeles: SAGE.

Zaragoza, Alex. 2020. "Penn Badgley Doesn't Take Playing a Psychopath on 'You' Lightly." Vice (blog). January 3, 2020. https://www.vice.com/en_uk/article/z3bvqx/penn-badgley-interview-you-season-2-netflix.

9 Data analysis in practice

Data-scraping meets the Regency era: *Bridgerton* commentary on YouTube

WITH CLAIR RICHARDS

Method: data analysis in practice

This chapter introduces you to the process of data collection and data reduction in practice. Using the Netflix Regency romance *Bridgerton* as an example, we are tracing user comments posted underneath YouTube reaction videos to the show's widely discussed first season.

Research question

The research question for this case study is an almost philosophical one: How can data scraping tools help us find 'unexpected' audience responses?

Data collection

The data collection for this chapter is entangled with very practical questions – how and where to find data, how to export it from social media platforms to a research environment. To deal with the sheer number of social media posts about the first season of *Bridgerton*, two different 'scraper tools' are used to find, collect and extract comments. This form of data collection also comes with decisions: In this chapter, we will discuss why we chose (1) YouTube as a platform, (2) User comments on YouTube and (3) User comments underneath five specific reaction video channels on Youtube to explore questions of popular culture and consent.

Data analysis

To analyze the 'scraped' user comments, we manually coded the data, clustered and theorized them using a grounded theory approach.

DOI: 10.4324/9781003315421-13

Key concepts

The logic of *'cultural citizenship'*, formally, is in the ways in which sociality is framed to negotiate a sense of belonging and identity in today's world using everyday media use (Hermes 2020, 1). The reaction videos allowed viewers to enjoy commenting on *Bridgerton* by sharing their understanding of the world. In our case study, we found that gender, race relations and popular culture were key issues in this negotiation of belonging.

Christmas 2020, the first *Bridgerton* series 'dropped': Set in the Regency era – early nineteenth-century London – the show is based on a series of eight romance novels that one by one see the Bridgerton children happily married after a stormy romance. In initial reviews ahead of the series' premiere, *Bridgerton* was described as a mix between *Gossip Girl* (Warner Bros. Television, 2007–2012 and HBO 2021-ongoing) and *Pride and Prejudice* (BBC 1995 or Working Title Films 2005). The release of the series' first trailer on YouTube was a clear signal to audiences that *Bridgerton* would be presenting Regency era romantic fiction unlike anything that had been done before. Innovative in its aesthetic appearance and its treatment of race, *Bridgerton* was highly anticipated.

Produced by Shonda Rhimes, who is also behind *Grey's Anatomy*, *Scandal* and *How to get away with Murder*, *Bridgerton* is not only the first 'Shondaland' series exclusively produced for Netflix but also a global phenomenon. Apparently, a whopping 82 million households watched the series' first season in the first 28 days after its release according to *Fortune* magazine.[1]

Watching *Bridgerton* in numbers

Doing our math, we can calculate that when 82 million accounts tuned into the series for at least a couple of minutes, and viewed it for 625 million hours in total (and knowing that the first season consisted of 8 one-hour episodes), a sizable proportion of the Netflix accounts that tuned in watched the entire season. Had they all watched all of it, it would have come to 656 million hours of viewing time.

Of course, there is a difference between the popularity of series based on numbers and statistics – and actually *liking* the series. The first *Bridgerton* season produced a veritable 'storm' on social media. Clearly, not everybody was amused by how it reinvented historical drama: Tweets expressed outrage at the 'historical inaccuracy' of the casting choices. How could nineteenth-century English nobility be portrayed as racially diverse? Adding insult to injury, the classical sounding music was also 'fake': How could an Ariana Grande song, performed by an orchestra, seriously be used as a period piece of music? The range of topics and sheer number of posts – on Twitter and other social media platforms – is a methodological challenge for research on such an immensely discussed example like *Bridgerton*. How can we get access to the range covered by these discussions? How to find the interesting bits? This chapter offers an example of how data scraper (API) tools can be used in audience research – and what advantages and hurdles are connected to having huge data sets.

A brief technical excursion: API is an acronym for Application Programming Interface. Basically, an interface helps connect. In this case, the interface is a type of software that allows the accessing of data and interaction with other software. So, our search tool knows how to 'speak' with – for example – the software behind Twitter in order to collect data. Here, the data we were interested in collecting were user comments. Data scraping tools make the attractive promise to deliver 'everything' that has been tagged with #Bridgerton on a specific platform. That makes these tools something of a blunt force weapon: 'Everything' can be a lot. In this chapter on data analysis *in practice*, we are continuing the methodological considerations of data collection and data analysis as *connected* started in Chapter 3 – and apply the call for research as a continuous process of decision-making to *Bridgerton* as a case study. This involved deciding on (1) a platform to collect data and narrowing down (2) which specific data to scrape on that platform.

Data scraping, data reduction: finding your way through discussions

There are three key elements to how to use data-scraped material:

1 *Finding the right locations to 'scrape' (or collect data)*
The data need to be of interest – and this might sound more obvious than it is. Oftentimes a promising data set turns out to be disappointing – either in size, or content, or variety. For this case study, Clair Richards started collecting data on Twitter. Tweets on the first season of *Bridgerton* were easy enough to find using the

scraper tool Coosto – but these tweets did not feel very exciting. Apart from all the grumbling and a smaller number of tweets appreciating *Bridgerton*, there was not much. In other words, this was not the right location to 'scrape'.

A simple Google search suggested that YouTube was a much more interesting platform to find lively and emotionally charged discussion. This we know by simply checking titles and the occasional YouTube video, clicking from one algorithmically recommended 'reaction video' to the next. Getting a sense of the YouTube reaction videos of *Bridgerton*, we noticed that those made by men had the highest numbers of views and reactions. At the next level, we went deeper into the content of the videos and realized that these seemed to be more humorous than the less-watched and more pedagogical reaction videos made by women. As Regency romance is traditionally a genre associated with women readers, our interest was piqued by the men's reaction videos.

2 *Knowing when (and what) to reduce.*
The second element of working with data scraping tools is that it is all about data reduction. In audience research, generally, the options for finding data are legion – you could always do more interviews, organize more focus groups, explore more online communities. Data reduction is how we find focus. In the case of the *Bridgerton* 'data hunt' – that started as a project of two Research Master students in media studies – we hoped that the material would allow us to chart everyday media criticism as the performance of cultural citizenship. That is, we hoped that the material would show different kinds of deliberation of identity, representation, our 'cultural' rights and responsibilities and what kind of media culture most of us would benefit from.

The data collected scraping Youtube offered a wealth of options for our analysis to focus on: race; class; popular culture; cultural capital and, unexpectedly, discussion of rape and consent. Working with large sets of data always involves a lot of 'killing your darlings' – letting go of fascinating examples and ideas to find your core argument. As we have discussed in Chapter 3, understanding data collection and data analysis as connected, as looping, and going back and forth, allows you to adjust your central research questions throughout your research. This is something you won't necessarily see in the final paper or project. Usually, when this type of research is written up, it is presented as far more orderly than how it unfolded.

3 *Thinking with and through the data.*
Especially, with open access and free data scraping tools, there is only a limited number of places where comments are easily accessed. But

accessibility is not a good enough justification for using a specific set of data – nor will this help you in narrowing down this (potentially still extensive) set to fit the scope and timeframe of your project. Rather than simply following the affordances of technological tools, follow your intuition. As a trained researcher, curiosity can be your guide in navigating platforms and thinking with – and through – the data you find. Generally, in getting a sense of a specific platform, in reconnoitering the landscape, a 'hook' will present itself.

To validate such forms of data collection, it is good to do spot checks on other platforms. In other words, as you are deciding what data to collect and how to reduce them, do try to remain open to developments. For our project on *Bridgerton*, we checked TikTok as well as Facebook in addition to our initial searches on Twitter and (final decision on) YouTube. Doing such a 'recce' tells us whether the reaction videos on YouTube and the lively practice of commenting on them is unique to the platform or an example of a more widespread practice of 'tv talk'. While we saw a different kind of reaction on Twitter, open Facebook groups had similar discussions. As we had a tool to 'scrape' all the YouTube reaction videos comments we found and the videos themselves were interesting in their surprising logic (men rather than women leading discussion on what we thought of as a real 'women's genre'), we chose to go with analysis of YouTube comments.

Practical steps: using a YouTube scraper tool

1 Based on our initial overview of 'reaction videos' on Youtube, we selected five YouTube channels as the basis for our data collection.

2 Using the YouTube Data Tools developed by Bernhard Rieder in 2015, all YouTube comments related to these selected videos were extracted as data via the YouTube API v3. The data tool assembles all the information that comes with the online text (timestamps, user names).

3 The data were saved as network files in .gdf but convertible to .csv – which is compatible with Excel. While you can export the data to other analysis tools and software, we decided to work with Excel for easy labeling and sorting.

4 We worked with only the actual comments: 3500+ (197+523+923+56+2061) reactions. While creative minds can

see stories in user names, here they were not informative nor do YouTube comments offer enough information to build a profile of the identities of the commenters.
5 Moving from data collection to analysis, we manually coded using grounded theory. You can find more information on how to build a coding tree in Chapter 3.

Watching men watching *Bridgerton:* 'reaction videos' as a starting point for audience research

In our process of decision-making, comments to five reaction video channels made the cut – based on their popularity and their specific content: (1) *Blindwave*, four gamers who tuned in to *Bridgerton* and were amazed at what they saw; (2) *Jack Edwards*, a literary critic and PhD student with a well-subscribed channel who read the *Bridgerton* novels; (3) The *Pink Popcast* run by Josiah Rizzo and Benji Jones, two guys who love popular culture; (4) *Sean Thompson* who does reaction videos for games and was asked by his followers to give his views on *Bridgerton* and (5) *Josh Pray*, a comedian who was in awe of the sex-appeal of the series romantic hero, played by actor Regé-Jean Page. The YouTubers behind these five channels are viewers themselves, more or less familiar with the (Regency) romance or the series itself. As YouTubers, they recorded their experience of viewing *Bridgerton* for their viewers. With reaction videos, the 'audience' we are researching thereby becomes layered.

Jack Edwards' reaction video aligns with the Twitter community and makes clear how far-removed romance reading is from literature. 'After watching the Netflix adaptation of Julia Quinn's "Bridgerton" books I decided to read the first book in the series called *The duke and I* ... and it made me want to puke and die,' Jack Edwards tells his 572.000 subscribers.[2] They often agree in the comments underneath the video: 'Romance novels are trash' appears to be the consensus here. In relation to cultural citizenship, the reaction video and the comments could be useful for discussion of 'distinction' and 'cultural capital'. How does being critical of popular culture make you feel more secure in your own class position? Are you someone who can distinguish trash from quality and is, therefore, someone who has taste?

The *Pink Popcast* reactions are polished and professional and appear spontaneous and unscripted. Reactions are presented in a pink frame and combine full/half and quarter screen footage of *Bridgerton*. The two reactors are culturally literate, one is a fan of period dramas, the other less so. Both approach the performative aspects of their own viewing experience of *Bridgerton* with enthusiasm and understanding of Regency era drama. They augment their commentary with audio and video clips from other popular series and films. *Pink Popcast* are especially fans of the elderly 'Lady Danbury' ('the bad bitch in red'). Their observations about her point commenters to the importance of race:

> *I loved her speech to Simon, the Duke of Hastings: 'the king's love of the queen is why black characters are part of the court. They are only there on sufferance'.*
>
> *They also loved how she is dressed: 'that was the flyest outfit' (a red one). She is their 'spirit animal' and 'exudes black excellence'. She 'brings black girl magic to the show.' Indeed she does:).*

Josh Pray, the comedian, appears to be totally taken by the series' main romantic hero, the Duke of Hastings: 'I am freaking out over how hot Simon is, the Duke'. It takes 'labial fortitude', he suggests, to watch a guy as attractive as he. One of his commenters wants Josh to explain *Bridgerton*. Because of the color blind casting discussion, the commenter thought it was a show about race, but it turned out it wasn't. A perceptive question really as it underlines how making race present, stops the series being 'about' race. Race has become a simple given.

Blindwave and *Sean Thompson* are the 'furthest' away from a knowledgeable position, but still garnered notable attention with their reaction videos (also at the request of their followers). The *Blindwave* gamers dress up as Regency nobles (very funny) and then are shocked when Daphne, the heroine, not only refuses the suit of a prince but loses the clearly priceless necklace he gave her when she meets up with the Duke. Their reaction plays out side by side with the scene, as the video shows the scene that is analyzed as an insert while we watch the *Blindwave* gamers go: 'Aaarrggghh'. The comments make clear how this is a one-off, on-request forage into popular tv drama. *Sean Thompson*, from his gamer's chair, is the one who first spots the lack of consent when Daphne stops the Duke from withdrawing when they have sex. He is incapacitated from having imbibed too much. He does not want to sire children given an awful childhood but is outwitted by his wife who has finally caught on to how babies are conceived. Like the others, Sean Thompson has a great eye for detail.

While all 'our' YouTubers are men, they come in an intersectional variety of sexualities, ethnicities and educational backgrounds. As the YouTubers were an eclectic bunch, we expect their followers to also be a diverse group. This brings us to the second layer of our project: we read the comments underneath the videos and the occasional exchanges through the lens of 'cultural citizenship'. The logic of 'cultural citizenship,' formally, is in the ways in which sociality is framed to negotiate a sense of belonging and identity in today's world using everyday media use (Hermes 2020, 314). It is popular culture allowing discussion of what binds people. What do commenters have hopes for, and what are they upset or critical about?

The virtual popular public sphere: cultural citizenship in practice

The audience for watching reaction videos is varied. Their remarks tell us that some are subscribers, fans and regular viewers of the videos, while others are led to the reaction videos because they want to discuss *Bridgerton*. Watching the reaction videos offers a kind of mediated coviewing experience. The reaction videos perform numerous cultural and social functions and act as a virtual space for the exchange of information and ideas as audiences attempt to understand what they have seen and try to agree upon shared meanings. The comments are sometimes questions but more often the comment space is for emotional support, discussion, sharing and debate about *Bridgerton* and the reaction videos. The participatory nature of watching reaction videos on *YouTube* and the affective impact that this has on 'creative communities' evolve the YouTubers' and commenters' viewing experience into a rich source of information for research (Despain 2020, 339/340).

So, what is shared then? *Bridgerton* addresses provocative themes through the eight episodes of the first season. Looking for focus, the comments about sexual consent (was this rape?) are the most interesting. For one, this was not discussion of your usual television rape scene. There are no torn clothes or marks of violence on a woman's body, the way in which television drama has preferred to depict rape (Cuklanz 2000). In the case of *Bridgerton*, Daphne, the female lead character, takes advantage of her – by then – husband's drunkenness to 'have her way with him' in order to get pregnant. She had no clue about what makes women get pregnant when she married and only slowly realized that her husband was practicing anticonception by 'pulling out' before his climax. For a reader of the original novels, Daphne might be a Regency era heroine for taking matters in her own hands. She fights with all the means at her disposal against the automatic position of authority and agency that the men in her life have, from her brother's interference into her marriage prospects to her husband's control of their family planning. For those new to Regency romance, or perhaps because television as a medium presents a more literal picture, Daphne taking advantage of her partner became an issue – as we found in the reaction videos and the comments underneath them. In our data, interesting discussions of masculinity, race, class and gender privilege culminated in a debate about consent.

Layers and/of consent: detangling the *Bridgerton* comments

Our coding of the collected data consists of a series of levels: there is a first level in which historical accuracy and race are predominantly discussed. A second level discusses masculinity (with a specific focus on how handsome the men are). The third level in the material offers access to another kind of anger than in the first level. While the first level is about taste and how popular culture is a domain of the atrocious lack of it, the third level is invested in the value of popular TV drama. That value appears to be compromised by Daphne's actions.

Sean Thompson's on-demand review immediately notices how Daphne's conduct does not meet ethical standards. The context to his observation is the loathsome history of white women using black men while disavowing their interest and complicity. Thompson does not remark on this nor does he need to. Jack Edwards makes his reaction video a bit later. By then, Daphne's 'rape' of the Duke has been discussed more widely – and critique is less about larger sociocultural questions of race and justice than about the simple lack of quality in the books (and the series). The *Pink Popcast* – who love popular culture and are ready to defend romance novels and their coming to television – offer the most interesting reaction. Initially, they simply rooted for Daphne against the arrogant Duke who assuredly betrays her by not explaining himself to her or offering her a route to sexual knowledge and emancipation. 'Sorry,' they post: 'we didn't cotton on to the lack of consent but this is a problem'. Similar negotiations can be found in the comments underneath the videos

> *Yes. I've heard others comment that it's more of a reproductive rape. He consents to sex but he doesn't consent to reproduction. It'd be like a woman flushing her pill down the toilet instead of taking it or a man poking a hole in his condom.*

Other commenters too switched from the topic of race to that of rape and consent within marriage. After the *Pink Popcast* are alerted about 'the rape', they edited their reaction to the episode and include a video disclaimer that addresses the 'controversial sex scene'. They apologize for their immediate reactions to the episode and assert that they no longer agree with their own responses to the scene. The new video, in turn, provokes a lot of discussion. Commenters are by and large appreciative of the inclusion of the trigger warning and apology. They share their views and educate one another on the nuanced nature of this discussion. In this discussion, it becomes clear that a cultural void exists. On the one hand, there are personal morals and shared rights and responsibilities within a marriage. On the other hand, there appears to be no legal protection for men when faced with the sexual and/or reproductive aggression of women.

Pushing this contrast even further, not all commentors even agree with the label of 'rape' for this scene:

> *I love that you kept your genuine reactions in! I guess I'm in the minority but I don't see that scene as having anything to do with consent. But we live in hypersensitive times so I can understand the argument. See you next time!*

> *The disclaimer was definitely needed. Although the scene was extremely uncomfortable and they both were wrong to sleep with each other without telling the other person their true intentions. I feel like in the times the show is based in, there wouldn't be a lot of talk on rape*

One commenter uses a curious turn of phrase referring to Daphne's actions as being a 'hint of rape'. This demonstrates the existence of different scales of judgment when thinking about rape.

> *I wonder if u guys have an opinion on the last love scene where some people may term it as a hint of rape; cos like Simon was forced.*

Others have no difficulty judging what happened:

> *What he did was without a doubt wrong but that doesn't take away from anything she did... intent does not count at all... if you engage in a sexual act without consent from the other person then its rape...*

> *I think its toxic from both ends because its rape on Daphnes side in that scene*

There is also support and understanding for what motivated the actions of both of the protagonists in this scene. The Duke's life has not been easy. It does not seem fair either that Daphne had little choice.

> *I think it's difficult only because the society she lived in was basically ROOTED in a culture of rape.*

A thread running through these comments – and the reframing of the reaction – is the question whether the morals and rules of nineteenth-century England (in which *Bridgerton* takes place) were very different to those of today. Although these discussions are often vague, they do address what 'progress' would consist of. Are we now more emancipated? Has society become more equal? How to properly contextualize popular TV drama in order for it to become a valuable forum of discussion around questions of consent is at issue here.

Conclusion: how to tell a story with your data

After coding and clustering comments, we see two options emerge to tell a story about cultural citizenship: One such story could easily be about the value of drama (whether literature or popular culture). The other would be about reproductive aggression perpetrated by women. For our case study, we find this second story the more interesting one. Although soap opera offers examples of the 'bad' woman using her sexuality to blackmail men, reproductive rape by women has not been depicted in television or streamed period dramas (but see Byrne and Taddeo 2022 for a recent update on rape in historical drama).

Popular television drama becomes a field that allows for discussion of the idea of male consent and how men might feel and be violated. This is cultural citizenship in action: in and through our data, we are noticing the discussion of the rights and responsibilities of citizens – then and now. As commenters put it in a longer discussion:

> *Why is it any different that it's a man? You're saying it's rape had it been the other way round. I don't understand how it's one rule for one sex and a different one for the other. How can it be any different morally? Consent is consent.*

> *I don't get why a lot of WOMEN don't understand consent of all things. Its getting ridiculous.*

> *It very much is rape. If a man sneakily takes the condom off during sex that's rape. Or if a woman pokes holes in the condom beforehand. Because it is not the type of sex you were consenting to have. So yeah.*

> *It's really difficult. He has more knowledge about sex and he consented to the sex. What he didn't consent to was cumming inside her. But I guess consent also wasn't a big thing back then. Either way I appreciate them for putting the disclaimer. I just wish Netflix would have done something similar?*

The reaction videos and comments are an exceptional online space. They are safe spaces where there is both challenging discussion and comforting support. There is humor but also serious discussion. To us, the 'reactions' to the 'reaction videos' show that television continues to facilitate the exchange of ideas and the calibration of ethical and political codes.

Note

1 https://fortune.com/2021/09/27/netflix-most-watched-series-films-bridgerton/

References

Byrne, Katherine, and Julie Anne Taddeo. 2022. *Rape in Period Drama Television: Consent, Myth, and Fantasy*. London: Rowman & Littlefield.

Cuklanz, Lisa M. 2000. *Rape on Prime Time: Television, Masculinity, and Sexual Violence*. University of Pennsylvania Press. http://www.jstor.org/stable/j.ctt3fhk4n.

Despain, Kagen. 2020. "Fan Films and Fanworks in the Age of Social Media: How Copyright Owners Are Relying on Private Ordering to Avoid Angering Fans." *Brigham Young Law Review* 2 (9): 333–80.

Hermes, Joke. 2020. "Tracing Cultural Citizenship Online." *Continuum* 34 (3): 314–27. https://doi.org/10.1080/10304312.2020.1764776.

10 Collaborative autoethnography in practice

"You knock on my door": an insider-outsider view of Turkish soap operas and fan labor

Method

For this case study, we are employing collaborative autoethnography – an ethnographically inspired method that uses personal experiences and practices as a starting point to explore larger questions. Applying the 'lens of the self' to explore changing forms of fandom functions as a form of cultural critique as well: the academic reading of a cultural phenomenon. In this case study, the popularity of Turkish soap operas – also called 'dizis' – and the different forms of labor connected to 'translating' them for an international audience.

Research question

In the conversational mode of collaborative autoethnography, our research question became more and more nuanced throughout our conversation – taking shape from the (very broad and very personal) question "Are you a fan of this?" to an exploration of when fandom starts to become 'work'.

Data collection

In collaborative autoethnography, the past and present experiences of researchers working together are the research material. Of course, this requires a great deal of self-reflection, trust and openness. For this case study, we are not summarizing continuing and current debates about fandom, but use our own personal recollections of (not) being fans as a

DOI: 10.4324/9781003315421-14

starting point to explore how fan identities and practices appear to change in a post-television landscape. Our starting point for this is a conversation about (not) watching Turkish soap operas.

Data analysis

Even though the material used for collaborative autoethnography might appear quite personal and anecdotal at first glance, the researchers' memories and life stories around a specific topic are treated with the same objective and academic understanding as other forms of data. In practice, this means that recollections are discussed, analyzed and interpreted in relation to a larger sociocultural setting – moving from the personal to the public and political.

Key concepts

Cultural Critique starts from an understanding of culture as something that is never finished but constantly constructed and changing. In this constant construction, all forms of popular culture – even those considered marginal, unimportant or 'low culture' like soap operas – play an important role. For this case study, we are suggesting an understanding of the Turkish soap opera *Sen Çal Kapımı* as an entry point into changing forms of interaction between viewers in a global and infrastructurally fragmented media landscape.

Fandom: what being a 'fan' means might differ from person to person: does it mean supporting your favorite sports team in the stadium, or does it mean spending hours commenting back and forth on a social media post about your favorite television character? For some, fandom might be something public, shared and structured (like a fan club), for others something individual, personal and private. What most definitions of fans have in common, though, is a sense of engagement – of different cultural practices that function as a passionate engagement with popular culture.

One of us knows a little too much about Turkish soap operas (if you ask the other one), one of us knows significantly too little (if, in turn, you ask the other one). And yet, we had plenty to talk about as it came to *Sen Çal Kapımı* (2020–2021). These conversations about a Turkish soap opera that became something of a global cultural phenomenon in 2021 is the starting point for this chapter. As one of the case studies presented in this book as 'methods in action', between discourse analysis *in practice*, data analysis *in practice* and media discourse analysis *in practice*, this chapter might seem to follow no method at all – at least at first glance. But, as we will argue, one of us watching and one of us not watching Turkish soap operas is precisely what makes this example so productive as a case study: approaching a cultural phenomenon from an insider perspective and an outsider perspective challenges us to think about our own positions as viewers, researchers and – maybe – fans. Michael Stevenson and Tamara Witschge propose that we should start to talk about methods as something "in service of curiosity and as embodied, sense-making operations" (2020, 118). With collaborative autoethnography, we are taking this call quite literally – and explore how an openness to understand different experiences helps us to make sense of fandom in a changing global media landscape.

For those among you who, too, know too little about the series: *Sen Çal Kapımı* stars former Miss Turkey Hande Erçel as 'Eda Yildiz', an energetic university student and florist, who hates but pretends to be in a relationship with the successful but emotionally distant architect Serkan Bolat (played by American-Turkish actor Kerem Bürsin). Over the course of two seasons and a total of 52 episodes – each around two hours long – their 'fake' relationship turns into a real one. With different names and different job titles, this narrative premise is fairly common in Turkish soap operas: due to the strict rules to protect 'moral values' for Turkish media, the fake relationship plays with the promise of romance without actually having to show romance in action. For the same reason, the cliffhangers at the end of each episode tend to be 'almost' kisses – that are then interrupted. The next episode takes up the storyline again. The haters-to-lovers storyline allows for this to happen multiple times as the protagonists are entangled in small and not so small personal and professional dramas. Of course, this general setup will be recognizable to viewers of other soap operas from non-Turkish contexts as well. What makes this series so special, then, is the tension between its immense global popularity and limited global availability.

In 2021, the final episode of *Sen Çal Kapımı* became the most tweeted about finale in television history, even surpassing *Game of Thrones*. With almost 8.5 million tweets in a single day, the hashtag #sonkezsençalkapımı (#YouKnockOnMyDoorForLastTime) trended not just in Turkey, but in the United States, Latin America and Europe as well. The rise of Turkish television exports has been gathering attention for quite some time already. In 2013, the *Wall Street Journal* published an article that opened with:

Often slushy, kitsch and highly addictive, Turkish soaps have since 2008 become a staple in living rooms across the Middle East, North Africa and the Balkans; enjoying wild popularity in ostensibly traditional societies for their portrayal of modern life styles and relationships.[1]

In addition to recentering soap-operas as a crucial genre for (post)television, this more recent online success also points to the changing form of global fandoms. While streaming platforms like *Netflix* increasingly offer 'regional' content for global audiences as well, the distribution of Turkish soap operas is still mostly tied to individual national television networks. In Italy, for instance, viewers could watch the series on the free TV channel Canale 5, in Tunisia on the television network Hannibal TV. Still, these syndications are tied to specific countries, and specific television schedules not necessarily in sync with the online attention to the series and its emerging fandom. Not available via large streaming platforms, Turkish soap operas are subtitled by Turkish fans and made available for free to global audiences via YouTube and other open video platforms in the gray area between legal streaming and illegal pirating. In this case study, we are using our own experience of (not) watching Turkish soap operas to negotiate when fandom starts to become 'work' – and in doing so follow in the footsteps of an established line of research into the practices of fans.

"If you enjoyed this episode, please support": watching and working

A few seconds into the opening of the first episode, the text appears for the first time: "We need at least 10$ to translate the next episode", an overlay reads as Eda and Serkan dance in slow motion in the background. Similar versions of the same message appear throughout this (and all following episodes), tying the (necessary) work of subtitling directly to the (felt necessity) of keeping up with the romance between the two main characters. Keeping up with currently running, weekly soap operas like *Sen Çal Kapımı* requires a variety of fan practices that mostly remain invisible to 'non-fans': In the absence of established television networks broadcasting the newest episode – or broadcasting the newest episode *immediately* – other infrastructures have emerged. These practices – of following, waiting and watching, commenting and donating – are intrinsically linked to other practices as well. One episode of the Fox Türkiye show is two hours + (not counting commercials). Recording, potentially editing out the commercials, subtitling and uploading the episode to another platform – as well as announcing via social media groups that the newest episode is available – are all returning activities that take considerate amounts of time. Whether or not these activities should be remunerated then, pushed our conversations about *Sen Çal Kapımı* into a new direction: Is this still 'fans' doing things for other 'fans', or is this a business model? And does the answer matter to our own practices of (not) watching? To explore these questions, we are turning to a specific approach in cultural and media studies: cultural critique. Quite importantly, critique is not the same as criticism. In the very first issue of the academic journal *Cultural Critique*, both the journal's aim and the larger idea of what cultural critique is, are defined as approaching cultural phenomena as "products of complex historical and structural relations rather than as isolated, self-subsisting artifacts" (1985, 5). In other words: Cultural critique zooms out from the individual media object to explore larger structures of meaning-meaning. Here, this means that we will not be diving into the narrative, the aesthetics or the production of *Sen Çal Kapımı* (although there is a lot to say about all of these!). Rather, we see our conversations about the series as a starting point to explore the structures of fandom and fan labor around and beyond this example in a globalizing media landscape. With cultural critique as our approach, collaborative autoethnography as our method and *Sen Çal Kapımı* as our object (of conversation), this case study very much draws on our own experience and perception while constantly referencing back to a larger academic and popular discussion of what being a 'fan' actually means.

Close relatives? Soap operas, telenovelas and the Turkish dizi

We are referring to Sen Çal Kapımı as a *soap opera* in this chapter almost matter-of-factly, while the more accurate genre would be *dizi*. As forms of serialized drama, there are quite some similarities between the soap opera, the Turkish dizi and the telenovela. Rather than pointing to their stylistic differences – in terms of cultural origin, pacing, production and themes – we use 'soap opera' as an overarching term here to center the fans and fan practices connected to serialized romances on television. For soap operas, these have for a long time also been tied to their classification as 'low culture', something only to be discussed privately and with other avid viewers.

We grew up with German and Dutch soap operas, respectively, and are both familiar with American soap operas – privately and academically. At some point, we might have even considered ourselves fans of some of these. Case in point: as an academic fan (we will return to this term later) of *The Bold and The Beautiful*, about the glitz and glamor and gossip of the fashion industry in Beverly Hills, Joke Hermes was interviewed about her love of the series – and it's female 'villains' – by different news outlets in The Netherlands. One of the key points that kept coming back in our conversations about soap operas in general – and *Sen Çal Kapımı* in particular – was the underlying notion that fandom was meant to be *fun*. Neither of us would consider ourselves as a 'fan' of anything that's not, inherently, fun: we follow politics, but we are not fans of politics. Instead, our associations with 'being a fan' were commitment, and pleasure, and a sense of ownership of different characters and their storylines. All of these are, undoubtedly, a form of investment as well. An investment of emotions, of time. On occasion, this investment might of course also go too far – even for fans themselves. That the term 'fan' is related to being 'fanatic' is not an accident. In an overview of the history of fans (and fandom studies), Henry Jenkins highlights how models of fan audiences are

> stressing their active participation within their own networked communities, foregrounding their own creative transformations and ideological negotiations with mass media texts, and imagining ways they speak back to texts, producers, and fellow fans, asserting their own agenda about what kind of popular culture they want to consume.
>
> (14)

Still, these active practices of engaging with and transforming texts are still on the 'fun' side of things: done by fans for themselves, or by fans for other fans.

Neither of us speaks Turkish (well) – our interpretation of the romance between Eda and Serkan, and the colloquialisms that can be found in most Turkish soap operas, are all dependent on either the viewing experience or the sharing of cultural interpretations by other fans. This 'translation' takes two different forms: the more classic 'fannish' form is fans posting in online forums, on weblogs, social media sites or under shared videos to explain what specific expressions or actions mean in the Turkish context of the series. Or, in our case: one of us explaining what other fans had explained to her – some sort of fannish game of whispers. The other form of 'translation' is a more complex one in terms of labor: the subtitling, uploading and sharing of the newest episodes could be understood as another service to the larger fan community. The request for donations and the returning appeal "If you enjoy this, please support" complicates this understanding. In our conversations, acknowledging of this as a form of 'work' crossed the borders of fan practices into a sort of customer service. Importantly, for other fans (and fan scholars), these distinctions might be different, the line drawn somewhere else. What collaborative ethnography allows for is the contextualization of the personal. Other methods of data collection are less likely to bring the tension between the dependence on these different forms of translations and the unease of potentially exploitive systems to the surface. Talking about the complex process of watching Turkish soap operas outside of established television networks pointed us to the blurry boundaries in contemporary fandom between 'labors of love' and 'labor'.

Academic, fan, acafan? Working as a fan

Crucially, the question discussed here is not whether or not fans should be compensated for the labor they do for media producers and companies. In a research project about the video game *Fallout 3*, Ryan M. Milner discusses how "fans view uncompensated labor as a foregone conclusion" (2009, 491). The same sentiment – and inherent criticism of capitalist exploitation – returns in research on how fan art and fan fiction get commercialized or appropriated (cf. Goggin 2018). Similarly, fan scholar Henry Jenkins suggests that in the context of shared infrastructures and digital platforms, "a familiarity with fandom may provide an important key for understanding many new forms of cultural production and participation and, more generally, the logic through which social networks operate" (2010). Production and participation are crucial terms for our discussion of *Sen Çal Kapımı* as well – both as it comes to our own participation in this fandom, and the larger trends we are exploring with and through this fandom.

With this case study, we are interested in how the different practices connected to the 'unofficial' translation, sharing and watching of Turkish soap operas complicate the relationship among fans. Does financially benefiting from other fans contradict the idea of a community of viewers? In our logic of fandom as something 'fun', this seemed to be case: in our recollections of what we had done, or were willing to do, as fans, 'producing' something of value – or depending on this value – pushed fandom into something different. "If television shows are cultural products, then reactions to them are reactions to cultural constructs" (2015), write Toon Heesakkers, Ward van Hoof, Anne Jager, and Amanda Gilroy in an article that revisits Ien Ang's research on *Watching Dallas*. Thinking autobiographically about how our viewing of different soap operas has changed and continues to change foregrounds how, as audience researchers, we are also audience members and always affectively entangled with the examples we discuss. Thinking about when – and why – we have self-identified as fans point us to how we are happily embracing some practices of fandom, while distancing ourselves from others.

While we are only discussing *Sen Çal Kapımı* here, the popularity of individual *dizis* as well as their – usually – closed narrative loops back to an increasing demand of other soap operas to be recorded, subtitled and shared for international audiences. As one practical example: one of the Facebook pages originally dedicated to (and fittingly called) "Sen

Çal Kapımı English subtitles" now posts links to the newest episodes of other Turkish soap operas. The question of what to watch 'next' – after the (usually) happy end of one dizi – can be found in social media posts, video comments and online forums again and again. And, of course, this question also came up in our conversation: we both have vivid memories of 'final' episodes of soap operas we had watched before. Some were really the last episodes, some were simply the last ones we had watched. In both cases, we tended to not immediately watch another soap opera right after. However, there seems to be something about the format – maybe it's the reassuring romance? – of Turkish soap operas that allow viewers to move from one to the next almost seamlessly. After finishing *Sen Çal Kapımı*, you might want to watch *Ask Laftan Anlamaz* that follows the (you guessed it) haters-to-lovers story of the desperately unemployed college graduate Hayat – also played by Hande Ercel – and Murat, the absurdly rich heir of a fashion empire. In turn, the work of translation expands from the individual series – and a fandom for one individual series – to the genre as a whole. At the same time, this expansion turns the 'labor' of recording, subtitling and uploading series more and more into a business model. Ensuring the spillover of fans from one series to another becomes crucial in sustaining this model, which adds another dimension to our discussion of what being a fan means in this context.

Aca-fandom and the question of authority

The term 'aca-fandom' points to the challenge of being an academic and a fan at the same time. Reading popular culture against and through philosophy and theory has the potential of offering new insights about what it means to be a fan and participate in a fandom. At the same time, identifying as an aca-fan comes with both methodological and ethical questions – for instance, whether or not the experience of participating in a fan event can be used for academic research. Ideally, the 'aca' and the 'fan' part of your identity inform each other. This also means that your knowledge and emotional experience as a fan – and those of other fans – are as valuable as your reading of them from an academic perspective. Put quite bluntly: Just because you are an academic, you don't know best. Rather, as an 'aca-fan' you have the unique opportunity to analyze fan practices and discourses from an involved and engaged perspective.

Thinking about fandom as entangled with labor – from the perspective of two media researchers writing a book – also comes back to our work: is watching and discussing these soap operas still 'fun' for us, or has it become 'work'? This might be a question to ask yourself as well as you are thinking about media objects to (not) write about. And pushing this even further: does an identification as aca-fan assume an interpretative authority of popular culture? Fans and scholars ask different questions and produce different knowledges – even though these might sometimes overlap. Here, we return to methodological considerations: using collaborative autoethnography to talk about the experience of (not) watching Turkish soap operas forces us to acknowledge these questions – and maybe more so than a method like textual analysis or other ethnographically-inspired approaches would. If "fans have always been at the forefront of media industry transformations", as Roberta Pearson argues, understanding shifting fan practices is crucial for an understanding of a changing media landscape.

Conclusion

As a method, autoethnography employs the lens of the self. For our case study here, working together – two different 'selves', so to speak – allowed us to access two perspectives on *Sen Çal Kapımı* as cultural phenomenon. This shift from autoethnography to collaborative autoethnography still functions as a reflection on and from within the personal sphere, but the dialogical format forces us to acknowledge our own identification as an insider/outsider of this specific fandom. As Brianna Dym and Casey Fiesler argue,

> online fandom is a space that is at once both very personal and separate from all things personal, as people bring with them to fandom the parts that might not be welcome in their daily lives while also leaving behind connections to their real identities.
>
> (2018, n.p.)

For our case study, having identified as fans before is important – as is the willingness and openness to do so in front of each other. Talking about soap operas we had watched and loved in the past – and challenging our own recollections – makes us recognize the situatedness of our perspective. Triangulating these sometimes fond, sometimes embarrassing memories of fandom with our perceptions of Turkish soap operas points to a larger shift not just in fandom practices but media practices more generally. Throughout this case study, we have used our own positions as a viewer and a nonviewer, an insider and an outsider, as a starting point to explore what forms of labor are connected to fandom in a post-television landscape. And if you enjoyed this chapter…

Note

1 You can read the whole article by Yeliz Candemir here: https://www.wsj.com/articles/BL-250B-117

References

Ang, Ien. 2015. *Watching Dallas: Soap Opera and the Melodramatic Imagination.* Translated by Della Couling. London: Routledge.

Candemir, Yeliz. 2013. "Turkish Soap Operas: The Unstoppable Boom." *Wall Street Journal*, April 29, 2013, sec. Middle East Real Time. https://www.wsj.com/articles/BL-250B-117.

Dym, Brianna, and Casey Fiesler. 2018. "Generations, Migrations, and the Future of Fandom's Private Spaces." *Transformative Works and Cultures* 28. https://doaj.org/article/29130a2da9fd44979df53a7db01689bf.

Goggin, Joyce. 2018. "'How Do Those Danish Bastards Sleep at Night?'*: Fan Labor and the Power of Cuteness." *Games and Culture* 13 (7): 747–64. https://doi.org/10.1177/1555412018760918.

Heesakkers, Toon, Ward Van Hoof, Anne Jager, and Amanda Gilroy. 2015. "Watching 'Dallas' Again 3: Reassessing Ien Ang's 'Watching Dallas.'" *Transformative Works and Cultures* 19 (June). https://doi.org/10.3983/twc.2015.0649.

Jenkins, Henry. 2010. "Fandom, Participatory Culture, and Web 2.0 – A Syllabus." Henry Jenkins. January 9, 2010. http://henryjenkins.org/blog/2010/01/fandom_participatory_culture_a.html.

———. 2018. "Fandom, Negotiation, and Participatory Culture." In *A Companion to Media Fandom and Fan Studies*, edited by Paul Booth, 11–26. Hoboken, NJ: John Wiley & Sons, Inc. https://doi.org/10.1002/9781119237211.ch1.

Milner, R.M. 2009. "Working for the Text: Fan Labor and the New Organization." *International Journal of Cultural Studies* 12 (5): 491–508. https://doi.org/10.1177/1367877909337861.

Pearson, Roberta. 2010. "Fandom in the Digital Era." *Popular Communication* 8 (1): 84–95. https://doi.org/10.1080/15405700903502346.

Przybylowicz, Donna. 1985. "Prospectus." *Cultural Critique* 1: 5–6.

Stevenson, Michael, and Tamara Witschge. 2020. "Methods We Live by: Proceduralism, Process, and Pedagogy." NECSUS_European Journal of Media Studies, Jg. 9 (2020), Nr. 2, S. 117–138. DOI: http://dx.doi.org/10.25969/mediarep/15344.

11 Media discourse analysis in practice

Aren't we *Friends* anymore? Watching and rewatching the sitcom

Method

Discourse analysis focuses on text. We use it when coding transcripts. We also use it when analyzing how media professionals write, e.g., about what a show 'does' for its viewers.

Research question

What does watching reruns of older sitcoms teach us about humor changing over time?

Data collection

International (online) news items about the sitcom *Friends* (NBC 1994–2004, available on Netflix since 2016) published by established (online) media between 2015 and 2022 in English, Dutch and German. Drawing on the algorithmic connection between different articles, we supplemented a Google search with following the links embedded within individual articles.

Data analysis

The unique strength of media discourse analysis is that it allows you to map and theorize the key terms to which opinions and interpretations of a phenomenon relate. It allows for comparison across national and international contexts. In this chapter, it provides insight into what can and cannot be said about humor and situation comedy.

DOI: 10.4324/9781003315421-15

Key concepts

Humor can refer to simple entertainment – something being funny – but it can also offer forms of social critique. Humor can take many forms, from friendly amusement to biting satire which indicates the ludicrousness of institutions or persons with power.

Taste and distinction: taste is knowing what to like and what not, and to display this in behavior, how you dress or decorate your home. It is dependent on 'cultural' capital rather than financial capital. Distinction is how showing 'good' taste sets you apart from those with less taste (see also Chapter 2).

Introduction

The starting point for this case study was an article about the sitcom *Friends*, "21 Times 'Friends' Was Actually Really Problematic". It was published in 2018 by the digital entertainment and pop culture platform *Buzzfeed*. The article draws on comments posted by members of the integrated community platform about the sitcom. The call for community comments was posted underneath an earlier article by the same author that outlined those moments she herself found problematic. While not a very convincing kind of journalism, it flags how the humor in *Friends* – and maybe in the sitcom more generally – is not aging well. Genre is important here. Sitcoms offer controlled and orchestrated forms of humor made for the consumption of a (distant) television audience. In usually weekly, half-hour episodes a recurring cast deals with and resolves challenges through collective laughter after a minor or major disturbance of the status quo. The "redemption of popular beliefs" and restoring of the status quo is important (Marc 1992, 20). Sitcoms reassure us. And, sitcoms deal with what is and is not normal. They effectively police 'etiquette' rules.

Mintz says that: "The 'situation' of the sitcom is the interruption of (-) normality, attempts at coping with the intrusion or problem, and the resolution of it allowing for what we could call 'the return to norm'" (1985, 42). Laughter more generally has been described as an instrument of socialization: when we are laughed at, we know we are doing something wrong (Billig 2005). Collective standards for what is funny and what is not are important, therefore. No surprise that this will change over time. In the time-honored commercial practice of rerunning older media material though, we see an interesting social experiment unfold in which media professionals assess the work of their colleagues in television production and sales. Not only do they often invoke us, the audience, to make their point (interesting for an audience researcher), but they also reflect on social and cultural change.

236 Episodes of *Friends* in as many words

Friends premiered on September 22, 1998, at 'prime time' on the US-American network *NBC*. It became a particularly important sitcom. As the television landscape changed, established networks had to find ways to remain relevant. NBC's answer was to focus on an unusual narrative in the network's new leading situational comedy. *Friends* starts out with six main characters that remain constant throughout the whole show. Three male and three female characters who share family relations and a living situation or both. Following different career and life paths – some more realistic than others – the characters on *Friends* are 30-somethings in the city, navigating everyday challenges and their uncertain futures. Sandell argues for instance that:

> Friends does not offer an unproblematic endorsement of marriage-and-kids as a goal for young people in the 1990s: characters either have children but are not married, will give birth but will not be the parent, or are neither married nor parents.
>
> (1998, 144)

Nonetheless, the series ends with (apologies for spoilering a series that ended two decades ago) a very conforming narrative: Monica and Chandler are parents and move to the suburbs, the will-they-won't-they history of Ross and Rachel comes to a happy end and Phoebe starts married life with supporting character Mike. Joey, of course, leaves the last episode single – but with a chick and a duck and a sequel on the same network.

Reading articles about *Friends,* we quickly noticed both a generational and a temporal divide: there appears to be a difference between 'watching' and 'rewatching' *Friends,* between 'then' and 'now'. Our research question for this case study started out as something like this: how does humor change with time – and how does that change how we (re)watch sitcoms? As we decided to use media discourse analysis as our method, rather than another ethnographic or textual approach, this first open question zoomed in on the complex ways that journalists position themselves as viewers just like us and more than us at the same time. Usually written as a critique, the articles not only challenge the nostalgic undertone frequently linked to rewatching television from the 1980s and 1990s. They also point us to an underlying ideology within media commentary as it comes to taste, distinction and humor at different moments in time.

"I'll be there for you…": the sitcom as form of belonging

Lawrence E. Mintz said that "it is hard to take sitcoms seriously" (1985, 42) but that we should try to do so nonetheless. Barlow and Westengard point out that situation comedies are "often entwined with our earliest memories, defining the ways we look back at our childhood and setting the terms of how generations see themselves" (Barlow and Westengard 2018, xi). Popular media texts such as the sitcom shape our individual perspectives but are also meaningful more broadly to communities and cultures. *Friends* is a case in point. The series' humorous, relativizing look at modern life, its setting in "private or leisure places, rather than work or public ones" (Sandell 1998, 145), the familial bond and self-referentiality of the characters made *Friends* a ground-breaking success.

The success of a sitcom is dependent on the success of its humor. So, what *makes* a sitcom funny? According to Giselinde Kuipers (2001), differences in the appreciation of humor are socially and culturally determined. Humor as a successful exchange of jokes and laughter is connected to taste. Humor requires cultural knowledge. When you laugh while others are not laughing or when you are not laughing while everybody else is, you will feel like an outsider (Kuipers 2001, 1). Humor can change social and moral boundaries into live wires. A person's social environment and background are important here– what people think is funny varies from culture to culture and from group to group. Contexts of time and place will determine how laughing with others will broker a connection.

Why do we want to be friends with *Friends*? Urban sitcoms and modern belonging

What we could call the 'urban comedy' frames the experiences of the sitcom characters in a broader societal change. Michael Tueth argues that "the scripts for these urban comedies have displayed new patterns of comic characters, relationships, plot resolutions and, in their effect on the larger culture, a new code for interpreting life in the 1990s" (2000). Outside of the living room and the office as the frequent focal point of earlier sitcoms, new places emerged as the center of the narrative: the café 'Central Perk' in *Friends* (NBC 1994–2004), 'Café Nervosa' in *Frasier* (NBC 1993–2004) or even more recently the 'McLaren Pub' in *How I Met Your Mother* (CBS 2005–2014). This move into the public sphere also relates to a shift in the relationships of the characters. Sandell argues, for instance, that *Friends* is "self-conscious about the construction of alternative kinship networks in the face of the alienation and despair of modern urban life" (1998, 143).

The last episode of *Friends* aired in 2004. Impressively, it has remained one of the most-watched shows on television networks and streaming platforms. In the *Wall Street Journal*, series cocreator Marta Kaufman said that the series' tone explains this: "It's not dark, it's not twisted, it's not about corrupt people. It's comfort food" (Flint and Sharma 2019). At the same, this comfort food appears to be increasingly difficult to swallow when we look at discussion of the show across English-language, German and Dutch media. Such media debates, comments and critique, in turn, become a reference point for audience members as they discuss how humor walks a fine line between harmless and hurtful, entertaining and problematic.

Rachel and Ross and Monica and Chandler and Joey and Phoebe and ... you?

As a critical viewer of *Friends* – or other sitcoms from around the same time – you might have had a similar experience. From today's perspective, some of the jokes don't seem very funny while they must have been funny before. Tracing media discourses about *Friends* (as an example of a globally popular sitcom) allows us to look at a long timeframe and a broad international context. We see that discussion of the sitcom appears to drastically shift over the course of the past decade. At the beginning of 2015, all 236 episodes of the sitcom became available on Netflix. While reruns of episodes of *Friends* had been quite common on television networks in the United States and elsewhere, the possibility to 'binge-watch' the entire series ushered in a rediscovery of the sitcom and then a dampening realization that 1990s humor was painful. There is fat shaming, homophobia, sexism, all in the name of a good punchline that restores what is and is not 'normal'. The shift from the comfort of being part of the *Friends* family to the discomfort of some of the series' jokes appears to take place around 2015 and 2016. Headlines shift from "11 Reasons why I'll watch ... again and again" (Lackey 2016) to "Is the humor of *Friends* outdated? Millennials find the series sexist and homophobic" (Ockers 2018).

Whether or not millennials really think so could have been the focus of a research project using focus groups or long interviews – then, in 2018. What would be much more difficult, however, is following the move from entertaining to offensive as we are doing through media discourse analysis over the span of ten years. In addition to the practical challenge of keeping interviewees engaged over such a long period of time, you would only be able to write about your findings at the end of this extended interview period. In most cases, you won't have that much time before the deadline for a research paper or project. Especially because news media are either archived and accessible via online databases or already digital in the first place, a methodological approach like media discourse analysis can allow you to look at the past from the point of now – in 2016, 2018 and 2023. Similarly, it would be much more difficult to compare how these discussions unfold across different contexts – especially in a smaller research project. Drawing on media discourses, we found that this was quite insightful though.

Everyday meaning-making changes with time, and with context. Two articles from our data set illustrate this well. The first is written by Isabel Ockers and published in the online version of the Dutch women's magazine *Linda* in 2018: "Is the humor of *Friends* outdated? Millennials find the series sexist and homophobic". The other one, "Racist, sexist, homophobic – why millennials can't laugh about *Friends*", is written by Tim Sohr and published in the German online magazine *Stern*. The titles suggest a similar argument. The Dutch article, however, lists the points of critique made by online viewers in a neutral overview of changing sentiments while the German article is a critique of 'oversensitive' viewers. Seeing these two articles next to each other highlights how discourses about taste and humor play out to different sets of norms. This is the unique strength of media discourse analysis: it allows you to see how a series comes to be interpreted in a new way (new terms are used), map how terms and adjectives change (from 'funny' and 'warm', to 'painful' and 'sexist'), while getting a better sense of how contexts matter (both of time and of place) and different sets of norms can be built from the same set of key terms.

Data collection: where to find THE news?

For this case study, we chose the route of convenience and used the search engine Google – and more specifically, the 'News' function of Google. As we were interested in media discourses in different national contexts, we used search terms in different languages in addition to the main keyword 'Friends'.

Depending on what you are interested in (and have access to), you could also conduct this form of data collection in an archive. Most libraries have an archive of local, regional and sometimes also national and international newspapers. Increasingly, the larger national archives are also accessible online and allow you to search in their collection without getting your hands dusty. For example, *Delpher* gives you access to Dutch historical texts from the digital collections of academic and heritage institutions and libraries. The platform *Europeana* has digitized newspapers from 20 European Countries published between 1618 and 1996. And some newspapers have also digitized their own archives: The *New York Times*, for instance, allows you to browse all issues from 1851 to 2018.

Another option to find relevant news items are archiving sites like *Nexis*. In addition to the inclusion of historical as well as contemporary news articles, Nexis allows you to limit the search results across a variety of parameters including language, location and timeframe. Compared to our Google search, this would allow you to finetune your search more strategically. The archive is not free to use but integrated into many university library systems and also offers solutions for businesses and market researchers.

Practically, media discourse analysis begins with and depends on sound data gathering. As does all audience research, actually! Search keywords were easy in this case: the term 'sitcom' has been adopted in Dutch, German and in other European languages. The same goes for *Friends* as the official name of the show across different national contexts (different to, for example, a drama like *La Casa de Papel* that is called *Money Heist* in English and *Haus des Geldes* in German). As we are most comfortable with English, German and Dutch, we used search results in these languages for our data collection. Following up on initial finds led us to more publications in these three languages. For each of them, we sought to reach saturation and then validated the search by using terms from individual articles. This is another recurring consideration of any form of research – and something that you will get better at the more you do it: knowing when 'enough' data are enough to tell a story!

"…when the rain starts to pour": changing times and changing meanings

At the same time, our data here show how journalists navigate their own position in these discussions of belonging and taste. In 2019, ahead of the sitcom's 25th anniversary, BuzzFeed News reporter Scaachi Koul dryly summarizes: "Here's the thing — this show has always been awful". Under the headline "*Friends* Hasn't Aged Well", Koul draws on her own position as a viewer of the sitcom during its original run ("someone who lived through the first round of *Friends*' cultural reign, who was conscious for at least half of it, and who participated in it in real time"), to problematize both the premise and the humor of the show ("*Friends*, a show about white people being thin and having the pointiest nipples in the continental Americas — and a show that I, at one time, watched and enjoyed — is absolute garbage"). In this example, you can already notice the dissonance between watching the sitcom then, and (re)watching it now – between what was funny then and what is funny now. Humor does not age well appears to be the consensus in the professional news items we analyzed for this case study. And this consensus is reached based on the private – but published – experience of individual media professionals.

As our perception of what is the norm, what is transgressive and what is acceptable changes, so does our understanding of humor – as the media professionals we draw on in this chapter point out. Take for instance the jokes directed at Chandler's transgender father ("Don't you have a little too much penis to be wearing a dress like that?"), or the fact that 'young Monica' was fat shamed ("I don't want to be stuck here with your fat sister") or the scene in which Ross asks what his son is doing with a Barbie doll. Once you start noticing these storylines, it is hard to not keep noticing them (cf. Woodward 2018a, 2018b for an overview of these moments). Laughing along with the laugh track becomes painful. In addition to thinking about how unfunny these moments seem from the present, media reflection on *Friends* also challenges whether the sitcom was funny to begin with.

Laughing alone?

In the early days of television, sitcoms were recorded in front of a live audience – and the live laughter was also audible to the audience at home. In addition to feeling part of an audience, a community of viewers, even while you're alone in your living room, the lived laughter signals that it's 'safe' to laugh, even about other people's misfortunes or transgressions. At the same time, this signaling potentially closes down alternative readings of the text (cf. Bore 2011). Does the viewer actually laugh because it's a good joke – or because laughing is the expected (and only accepted) reaction?

And yet, there seems to be more to a sitcom like *Friends* than just its funniness. Humor extends an invitation to belong – and having once 'belonged', second-time viewers appeared to seek that feeling again. Nostalgia, our media material suggests, is an important motive for going back to *Friends*. Kevin Reilly, the chief content officer of HBO Max and responsible for *Friends: The Reunion*, emphasized that the series "taps into an era when friends – and audiences – gathered together in real time and we think this reunion special will capture that spirit, uniting original and new fans" (Tobler 2020). Exploring how the nostalgic longing for comfort television and the critical discussion of problematic tropes returns in the media discourse around *Friends* points us to understanding humor as a practice of belonging and inclusion, and laughing (together) as a matter of taste.

Conclusion: 'Impromptu' audience research?

Most of the articles we found are opinion pieces – and as such explicitly position themselves as representing the 'trained' opinion of entertainment writers, pop culture journalists and television critics. As evidence, these professionals draw on two kinds of evidence:

1 *Their own experience as viewers, reminiscent of autoethnography.*
One of the recurring subheadlines of the news articles is a version of "Thoughts I had while watching *Friends*" – which points to an understanding of the journalist's experience as representative of larger cultural sentiments, shared with other viewers.
2 *The experiences of other viewers, in the form of selected online comments.*
A surprising number of the articles we read reference 'non-professional' discussions – on Twitter, on Reddit, on integrated discussion boards, and most recently on TikTok – as support for their claims.

As we are moving toward the end of this book, you will not be surprised by our issue with this: neither form of evidence convinces as audience research. There is no reflection on their data collection, and no making sure that their choices in what makes it into the article – and what doesn't – are visible and justified. Although a 'theory' is produced, this is theory in the loosest sense. While more than a hunch, it is an assemblage of arguments that is meant to provoke and entertain rather than be a testable argumentation for which the author has also sought counter-evidence. In practice, the key difference is that we usually see little of the contradictions and paradoxes that surface in qualitative audience research.

Media discourse analysis shows something else as well. As online discussions are taken up and reframed in other news media, a layered intertextuality is produced that suggests more unified and polarized groups (Fiske 1987; Hiramoto and Park 2012) than you might find with and through other ethnographic methodologies. When audiences are presented as a collective in news media, individual differences are obliterated, and issues are further politicized. Watching a sitcom-like *Friends*, then, becomes not just a question of humor and taste, but of larger cultural sensibilities – and of falling short of those. "You can't really find this funny, can you?!", these articles seem to suggest through their representation of a collective and unified response to the sitcom from today's perspective.

While a lot has changed in television over the last decades, at least when looking at the genre of the sitcom, a lot also seems to have remained the same. If humor is – following Giselinde Kuipers' sociology of humor – both socially and culturally shaped and dependent on time and place, looking at current trends like reboots, remakes and revivals is especially interesting as it comes to our relationship to the settings, characters and relationships in sitcoms. Tracing the changing sentiments about what of a sitcom like *Friends* is acceptable and what isn't through media discourse highlights larger negotiations about shared understandings of norms. The continuing success of sitcoms across channels and platforms emphasizes that comedy continues to play an important role for television – even if that role might be changing. The last episode of *Friends* ended with Ross, Rachel, Monica, Phoebe, Joey and Chandler leaving the keys to their well-known and well-loved apartment behind on the kitchen counter of the empty room – to head where they started off in the show's opening sequence 236 episodes earlier. Thanks to perpetual reruns and remakes (that in turn become reruns), we can always return to watching them. Whether we will like what we find is a different question, though ...

References

Barlow, Aaron and Laura Westengard, eds. 2018. *The 25 Sitcoms That Changed Television: Turning Points in American Culture*. Santa Barbara, CA: Praeger.

Billig, Michael. 2005. *Laughter and Ridicule: Towards a Social Critique of Humour*. London: SAGE Publications Ltd. https://doi.org/10.4135/9781446211779.

Bore, Inger-Lise Kalviknes. 2011. "Laughing Together?: TV Comedy Audiences and the Laugh Track." *The Velvet Light Trap* 68: 24–34. https://doi.org/10.1353/vlt.2011.0011.

Fiske, John. 1987. *Television Culture*. London ; New York: Methuen.

Flint, Joe, and Amol Sharma. 2019. "Netflix Fights to Keep Its Most Watched Shows: 'Friends' and 'The Office.'" Wall Street Journal, April 24, 2019, sec. Business. https://www.wsj.com/articles/netflix-battles-rivals-for-its-most-watched-shows-friends-and-the-office-11556120136.

Hiramoto, Mie, and Joseph Sung-Yul Park. 2012. "Media Intertextualities: Semiotic Mediation across Time and Space." In *Benjamins Current Topics*, edited by Mie Hiramoto, 37:1–10. Amsterdam: John Benjamins Publishing Company. https://doi.org/10.1075/bct.37.01hir.

Koul, Scaachi. 2019. "The One Where We Talk About How 'Friends' Actually Sucks." *BuzzFeed News*. August 29, 2019. https://www.buzzfeednews.com/article/scaachikoul/friends-anniversary-bad.

Kuipers, Giselinde. 2001. *Goede Humor, Slechte Smaak: En Sociologie van de Mop.* Amsterdam: Boom.

Lackey, Emily. 2016. "11 Reasons I'll Watch 'Friends' Again & Again." *Bustle.* March 16, 2016. https://www.bustle.com/articles/148437-11-reasons-ill-watch-friends-again-again.

Marc, David. 1992. *Comic Visions: Television Comedy and American Culture.* Repr. Media and Popular Culture 4. New York, NY: Routledge.

Mintz, Lawrence E. 1985. "Ideology in the Television Situation Comedy." *Studies in Popular Culture* 8 (2): 42–51.

Ockers, Isabel. 2018. "De humor in 'Friends' over datum? Millennials vinden de serie seksistisch en homofoob." *Linda*, 2018. https://www.linda.nl/persoonlijk/humor-friends-datum-millennials-vinden-serie-seksistisch-en-homofoob/.

Sandell, Jillian. 1998. "I'll Be There for You: Friends and the Fantasy of Alternative Families." *American Studies*, June, 141–55.

Tobler, Jeff. 2020. "The One Where They Got Back Together | Pressroom." February 21, 2020. https://press.wbd.com/na/media-release/hbo-max/one-where-they-got-back-together.

Tueth, Michael V. 2000. "Fun City: TV's Urban Situation Comedies of the 1990s." *Journal of Popular Film and Television* 28 (3): 98–107. https://doi.org/10.1080/01956050009602829.

Woodward, Ellie. 2018a. "What Are the Most Problematic Moments in 'Friends?'" *BuzzFeed.* March 14, 2018. https://www.buzzfeed.com/elliewoodward/what-are-the-most-problematic-moments-in-friends.

———. 2018b. "21 Times 'Friends' Was Actually Really Problematic." *BuzzFeed.* March 16, 2018. https://www.buzzfeed.com/elliewoodward/times-friends-was-actually-really-problematic.

12 Ethnography versus focus group research in practice

Sports talk: watching, feeling and connecting

Method

As a starting point to explore how media(ted) sport is connected to feeling – both in the moment and in general – this chapter introduces you to three research projects using focus groups and interviews centered on fans of the Dutch National Soccer Team. Following on 'existing' examples, this chapter proposes a few entry points for your own audience research project using the 2022 World Cup in Qatar – and the surrounding controversy – as a case.

Research question

The research question for this chapter is a very broad one and could go something like this: how does sports make us 'feel'?

Data collection

As an example for ethnography in practice, we are introducing you to the research of Jacco van Sterkenburg (2013 and 2019): in his research, a discourse of 'enlightened racism' comes through in sports talk. The irony that race and ethnicity do not matter when you perform well is not lost on informants and especially not on those with a non-white ethnic background themselves. This, of course, is only one dimension of what sports can make us feel – but it does point to larger questions of identity and belonging.

Data analysis

Starting with focus groups, the example project balances between an inductive and a deductive approach. Inductive is to learn and theorize from

DOI: 10.4324/9781003315421-16

a small number of observations, cases or examples. Deductive is to test a hypothesis. Overall, though, this is an inductive project in that it uses a grounded theory procedure to analyze the data.

Key concepts

Emotion is the social performance of feeling. It starts from experiencing consciousness or a bodily sensation. Emotions run the gamut from positive to negative: happiness, sadness, disgust, anger elation. Emotions are often seen as the opposite of rationality and thought. Sexism (the ideology that denigrates women) defines women as 'emotional'. Then it means: showing too much feeling.

Affect is how we are 'touched' by the world, what moves us and circulates between people in societies rather than what we feel 'inside' ourselves. Love and hatred are good examples when taken to the social level: white supremacy is based on hatred as affect, fandom on love. Affect can be described as how feeling circulates and is stored ideologically and materially.

Cultural Racism is a prejudiced worldview based on understanding ethnic and racial groups to be different. Contrary to biological or scientific racism it understands cultures to be fundamentally different with some superior to others.

Sport is television's oldest content. For good reasons! Think of the excitement of unpredictable outcomes, week after week, match after match. The closely filmed exertions of athletes and their bodily abilities are highlighted in close-ups and more close-ups. The excitement of a match point, the awesome tactical insight of top team players. As viewers we can temporarily, in our imagination, co-own representing 'our' nation, 'our' team or 'our' club. We can be deeply moved by pride and joy or by commiserating with athletes experiencing burnout. Whether we hear about Dutch cyclist Tom Dumoulin prematurely ending his career or top athlete Simone Biles saying 'no' in the Tokyo Olympics in 2021: we feel with them. As Raymond Boyle puts it: "The way these stories are delivered, and are made sense of by audiences in the digital age, variously reflect, reinforce and construct a range of identities around class, gender, ethnic and cultural and national identities" (2014, 747). Through its emotional stories, sport has an almost unrivaled capacity for community building.

Sport enters our lives in different ways and in different places. Most of the time, sport is also related to evaluation – of performance and of behavior, by (sport) media professionals and viewers – and our feelings about these evaluations. And sport, different from other media content, is excessively talked about. Most of us, fan or not, will be aware when big sports tournaments are played. They enter media spaces in the form of live matches, commentary, summaries on the evening news, memes and jokes. They set in motion expert discussion, dissection of tactics and strategies as much as nationalist feelings. They inform what we talk about and with whom. Professional athletes often function as 'moral examples' on and off the field, and the absolute opposite when they don't pay their taxes, cheat on their partners or are involved in drunk driving (Hermes 2005; Jorge, Oliva and Aguiar 2021; Whannel 2000). This chapter explores how ethnographic methods point us to how sport talk 'feels'. Rather than offering one individual methodological approach, we will use one type of mediated sport event – soccer tournaments – to show how audience researchers can capture the emotionally charged side of sports. On and off the field!

The liveness of soccer meets live television

For this chapter, we are focusing mainly on tournament soccer – not necessarily because this is the sport we both enjoy most but because live soccer and live television have a special relationship. Other sports are easily as interesting and deserve more attention than they are usually given. However, no other live television has captured as many viewers worldwide as soccer championships have, apart from the funeral of the British Queen Elizabeth II in 2022. Her coronation in many ways marked the start of broadcasting television. Her death may well signal broadcasting's enduring power to capture us.

To understand audiences' love of mediated sports across its impressively diverse feats, failures, exceptional figures and emotional experiences of fans and non-fans, we need methods that do very different things. If we want to come closer to the excitement – the affective dimension – of sports spectatorship, participative methods work well.

- How sport unites (and divides) can, for example, be researched through *focus groups* that allow for comparing groups with one another
- With common phrases like 'our' team and 'our' win, sport – and that includes mediated sport – capturing and constructing identities. In *interviews*, you can trace how these constructions evolve with and through new experiences of sport

- *Sensory ethnography* can help capture feelings of euphoria, community building and recognition. Or distaste for the uncouth behavior of fans, or the extensive claim a major tournament will put on our collective attention)

The strength of all participative methods is that they allow you to address *multiplatform* content, from traditional broadcasting and its use of statistics and game analysis, to shared social media snippets and stories, to gossip and sensational news sites, to memes drawing on a match (and its players) long after the final whistle. Below, we will first connect the threads of an older audience research project on televised World Championship soccer that uses focus groups and long interviews to reconstruct shared feelings about the Dutch National Team, to then explore how the recent FIFA Soccer World Cup 2022 could become a good topic for a (small) research project.

Soccer stories: the connection between viewing and belonging

Whether or not you are a fan of soccer, you will likely be able to tell a 'soccer story': it might not necessarily be a specific match you remember, but a player's unique style (in sports or fashion) or a viewing practice that stuck in your mind. Or how you celebrated the World Championship win of 'your' team. In all of these examples, sport is similar to but also fundamentally different to other types of fandom. While it does create strong allegiances (similarity), it connects these with cultural and political identities (difference). Winning or losing, watching or not-watching, then, becomes much more than a media practice. Which adds another element of sports talk: its investment in statistics and achievements. It has transformed accountability into entertainment that has the added advantage of distinguishing the 'real' fans from hangers-on. What does one need to know, or need to 'do' to be considered a fan? And, do you really 'feel' with and for your team?

For most research projects, you will likely begin with an overview of existing research. A literature search on, e.g., Scholar Google would point you to two articles by Jacco van Sterkenburg published in 2013 and 2019. The first one is entitled 'National bonding and meanings given to race and ethnicity: Watching the soccer World Cup on Dutch TV'. The second one focuses more generally on how soccer media and racial and ethnic stereotypes are relevant to young audiences (Sterkenburg, Peters and Amsterdam 2019). In both cases, his interest is in how race and ethnicity matter in how Dutch fans talk about sports and how that connects to larger questions of belonging. Let's look more closely at these projects to tease out the strengths of focus group research and perhaps also its pitfalls and weaknesses.

Learning from existing research: how to describe your methodological approach well

'The interviews were structured around three topics: (1) participants' connectedness with the Dutch national soccer team during the 2010 World Cup, (2) the role participants' ethnic identification played in their support for (players of) the Dutch national soccer team and (3) participants' evaluation of Dutch soccer commentary and sport commentary generally, and their own discourses surrounding race/ethnicity. The interviews were literally transcribed and then analyzed by a search for emerging themes and patterns. This openness to the data is typical of a grounded theory approach, in particular of the initial process in this analysis called open coding. Characteristic of open coding is the breaking down of the interview data into separate units of meaning that are labeled identically if they refer to the same phenomenon' (Sterkenburg in *Soccer and Society* 2013, 390).

Such a description could well introduce the coding tree. The third set of codes toward the top of the tree (called selective codes, or themes or interpretative repertoires, see *Chapter 3*) could then be used as labels for sections in the paper written about the research project, or as names for chapters in a thesis.

Generally, qualitative audience researchers know that saturation (the moment when collecting more data does not deliver any new information and insights) is reached fairly quickly. A well-curated sample of interviewees (women, men, different ethnic and class backgrounds) will have a very high probability of covering the social logics of sports talk. In the 2019 project, Sterkenburg focused on the differences between young Dutch women and men, while taking into account a broad range of racial and ethnic differences. The underlying assumption is that intersections matter in identity construction: to be a young Dutch-Moroccan woman offers a very different set of opportunities and challenges than to be a young Dutch-Moroccan man. An ethnographer might well object and argue that it is important to start from 'members' categories' and therefore to not sort informants under identity labels beforehand but to ask how they identify themselves. It is entirely possible that such an approach would have been less efficient. It would have taken more time to do participant observation and have informal conversations before being able to ascertain whether and how identifications were a matter of giving socially desirable answers or, indeed, how informants see themselves. Dutch-Moroccan Amsterdammers, for instance, would identify as Amsterdammers or even by their neighborhood's postcode rather than by nationality. Would they have had different things to say in terms of what Sterkenburg and coauthors call the hegemonic constructions of race and ethnicity in relation to sports? Quite possibly not. We would perhaps have gained a better understanding of why enduring racisms make so much sense locally. The local identification is important in that it enables a variety of national allegiances that do not counter how (young) Amsterdammers feel connected to their (diverse) neighborhoods. In the 2019 project, Sterkenburg and his coresearchers invited 36 people (both women and men) into focus groups that consisted of White Europeans, Surinamese or Moroccan Dutch (his labels). By dividing his informants in three groups, Sterkenburg tests the hypothesis that nationalist allegiance does (not) play into the emotional and evaluative experience of watching world cup soccer. Comparing these three focus groups shows what tricky concepts nation and nationalism are.

Soccer feelings: experiencing sport in the everyday

There are multiple entry points to think about mediated sports from an audience perspective: observation and participant observation play with the 'liveness' of viewing practices. Short interviews, long interviews or group interviews before, during or after tournaments point to the embeddedness of sports in everyday media and could also zoom out from individual matches to sports programs in general. What defines winners and losers and heroes for viewers? Some of these discussions could also be followed via online discussions and online forums: What are the pleasures of soccer strategies and tactics, and what constitutes quality and potential? And who gets to participate in these conversations? Autoethnography could allow you to become attentive to the multiple textual layers as experienced by viewers – including the commentary, the talk shows, the ads, the news in newspapers and on news websites, the podcasts, the predictions on dedicated sports websites by experts and viewers, the betting, the memes, the women's magazine tips and recipes for 'soccer night'.

Mediated sport events are much more than mere media content. They are a vehicle for identity, for community, for taste and knowledge, for gender(ed) performances as much as the ongoing commercialization of sports and the scarily enormous amounts of money that are involved. Sports is an industry in itself – as you can tell from the advertising on jerseys, tickets, the stadium. They are a rich source of gossip for old-fashioned gossip magazines, for the more recent 'juice channels' and for the celebrity culture that manifests itself in reality television shows as well as fictional series that portray the wives and girlfriends of soccer players (Kavka 2012). Barbara O'Connor and Raymond Boyle connect watching televised sports with watching soap operas through the analogy of 'Dallas with Balls' (1993). And talking about soccer might come in very different forms, too. This is also Joke Hermes' conclusion in even earlier work. She found that men use different types of technical talk: there is knowledge of the rules of the game, tactics, strategy and a type of knowledge that involves soccer statistics (the curricula vitae and achievements of players and trainers). Both types of knowledge were presented with a high degree of 'Miss Marple-ism', which Hermes also considers to be a kind of interpretive knowledge in itself. The men do not hesitate to reach far-reaching conclusions about persons. It is gossip, really, but presented as technical knowledge and insight. Interestingly, a link to racist discourses or to discourses involving skin color or cultural difference is only made when talk turns to the national team (Hermes 2005, 62).

Among the women she interviewed, a very different pattern emerged. They underlined that watching soccer together was a convivial way to spend time ('snug' or 'cozy'), to which they added, half in fun, a good way to watch men: 'Doesn't he have a cute butt?'. Although they too objectified the players' bodies, their sexualization was not in any way racialized or racist (Hermes 2005, 64). Such talk of sexy bodies would not emerge in more formal interviews, whether in focus groups or individual interviews. Informal and sensory-oriented forms of ethnography though turn more easily to the pleasures rather than 'serious' meanings of televised sports. An example like this would also open itself up to a link to textual or visual analysis: noticing more women as presenters, commentators or pundits on sports media could be a starting point to explore whether or not the male-defined world of televised world championship soccer is opening up to women. Or how sport overall has an impact on racialization due to the hypervisibility of bodies, especially of persons of color. An audience researcher would not necessarily need such a specific focus beforehand – although she would be noticing such things. She could simply start with the tried and tested audience research question: what is the 'pleasure' of sports for viewers? In due course, such a broad question leads to more focused ones and, in the end, usually, to stories that would have been impossible to predict beforehand.

In different types of sports talk, and the pleasure of it all, you can see the emotional component return as well. Talking to and with viewers about sports can then also point to how you – as audience researcher – want to talk about sports in turn. Whatever the ultimate choice of a topic, a good ethnography sets the stage for the story it wants to tell. For a project like Hermes', long quotes from participants function as a form of well-documented storytelling: they introduce the context of the research project and give a sense of how the story is built from 'scratch'. In the next section, we will turn to the 2022 World Championship as a potential case study. Between the politics of the decision to host the tournament in Qatar and the practical consequences for viewers in such mundane ways as the weather, viewing sport also always relates to feeling. This is where a sensorial ethnography could start. Indeed, literally with sports journalism's most asked silly question: How did it feel?

Hermann Bausinger on 'media, technology and daily life' (1984)

In 1984, the venerable journal *Media, Culture & Society* published a short essay by the German ethnologist Hermann Bausinger in translation. The meat of the story is an anecdotal example detailing Mr. Meier and how he negotiates his love for sports, or actually for his local club United, with sports media coverage. It is a funny story of avoiding hearing the outcome of the Saturday match before the televised summary, then missing the sports program, buying a sensationalist newspaper and being caught doing that by his son. Mr. Meier's sports fan routine makes for a good story that illustrates how rituals both structure everyday life and require attention and management.

Meeting Bausinger in the mid-1990s, he admitted with a smile that the Meier family example was a fictionalized rendering of his own 'sports weekend'. It shows there is value in fictionalized autoethnography and in forms of home-based participant observation. In the essay, his experience leads him to state six principles for media research

1 It is all about the media ensemble. 'Recipients' will integrate different media forms.
2 Media are not used completely or with full concentration. We cannot predict beforehand how they will be used in real life with all its distractions.
3 Media are an integral part of conducting our everyday lives. Are a surprising number of women watching a sports program:

it might be the appeal of the presenter or a wish to be together as a family, or something completely different.

4 Others are always important to our media use. Whether present or not, they hinder, challenge or encourage us.

5 Media contents are material for conversation. We talk about them.

6 While a text might be said to have an 'implied' reader, there is no such thing as an average or synthetic reader in real life. Media texts are far too ambiguous.

For more on sports' intricate relationship with technology and datafication, see Markus Stauff *A Culture of Competition: Sport's Historical Contribution to Datafication* (2018). With Carlos d'Andrea he also argued that "sports systematically fosters 'mediatized engagements with technology' that can productively expand and reframe the role of 'pioneer communities'. When sports audiences discuss the application of a new epistemological technology (and the respective TV coverage) on social media platforms like Twitter they articulate ideas about the qualities of this technology, its appropriate use on the field, in a specific match, and its broader (detrimental or beneficial) impact on the much beloved sports". The article tackles discussion of the VAR (the video assistant referee in soccer) on Twitter (Andréa and Stauff 2022).

Infamous soccer: researching the FIFA World Cup 2022 in Qatar

The decision to host the 2022 FIFA World Cup – one of the world's largest soccer tournaments both in terms of viewers and investment – in Qatar was a much debated one. FIFA, the Fédération Internationale de soccer Association, is not necessarily new to scandal and scrutiny: were the chief executives bribed (again) to allow the Arab country to host the game? Were politicians 'incentivized' to overlook Qatari politics and the country's seeming indifference to human rights? A shocking number of guest workers who built the stadiums, for instance, have fallen ill and died due to terrible working conditions. The country is not safe for LGBTQ+ athletes. Global North media discussed whether this tournament should really happen and a predictable discussion followed, to no avail. There was much discussion in public and private of whether to go to Qatar (with a national team) and whether to watch the matches (at home) at work, in cafes and in living rooms. All national teams that qualified, did go.

However, heated the discussions before, it made no difference to the viewing figures for the 2022 Qatar tournament in the Netherlands. The ratings were higher than ever. Money was made as per usual from different kinds of advertising: some around the field, some in separate blocks before and after the matches. And also as usual, it might have flowed not necessarily into the 'right' hands. As a starting point, the media(ted) talk of a boycott could make for a good research topic: newspapers and news shows published a lot of interesting and relevant material. Petitions circled online, as did 'behind the scenes' footage that highlighted the problematic context of the tournament. (Former) players, coaches and pundits also commented publicly before, during and after the World Championship actually took place. Some in favor, some against.

> NBCSports reported on the third day of the tournament that for the 2022 tournament in Qatar, the viewership is predicted to be five billion across the world, making that an average of 227.27 million per day (Sanjesh 2022). While these numbers are estimations – and not based on transparent and accessible calculations – they do speak to the importance granted to the World Championship in and outside of the media.

Ethnography is easily one of the most fitting ways to approach the complex negotiation of watching-not-watching, of boycotting-not-boycotting, of enjoying-but-guilty surrounding this specific championship. The distinctive and iterative format of gradual funneling and focusing on what exactly should be researched allows the researcher to follow discussion and practices as they play out in real life and real time. In practice, such a project would consist of several rounds of participant observation and interviewing:

- The starting points are the practices you observe and the conversations you notice around the World Championship. Are the 'usual' fans thinking about whether or not to watch? Are viewers less likely to go to public streamings? Is not-watching the games the same as not-keeping-up with the results? Do national or regional allegiances play into the emotional experience of (not) watching?
- Transcribed interviews, field notes and research memos would then be analyzed via summarizing and coding. The codes would help to come to a first sketch of the meanings and pleasures of international televised soccer tournaments, and the particular negotiations surrounding the 2022 tournament

- In a next step, these codes might lead to a focus on specific aspects, or specific audience groups or particular environments. Dedicated soccer fans, for instance. Or female viewers. Or public viewings. At some point, your research would reach saturation – this means that you feel that a meaningful story and perhaps new concepts are starting to emerge

Of course, interviews about these big tournaments can also be organized 'afterwards'. For soccer, they are biannual returning events in Europe, Africa and South-America, where regional cups (the biannual Africa Cup of Nations, the four-yearly Copa América or UEFA European Championship) interchange with the World Cup. How are the negotiations surrounding the 2022 World Cup informing how viewers think about where and when to host these tournaments? Do viewers feel differently about these events now? Why, or why not? A few conversation starters:

- *Soccer Federation Politics*: the head of FIFA, Giovanni Vincenzo "Gianni" Infantino, is rumored to plan an extra three-continents world cup with the emir of Saudi Arabia – is soccer all about money now?
- *National Allegiance*: the coach of the Dutch National Team, Louis van Gaal berated the press for always being critical of his team and its coach – should sports media have an allegiance to 'their' team as well?
- *Decolonizing Sport*: the participation and performance of the Senegalese and Moroccan national teams
- *One Rule, One Love*: national teams were forbidden to wear a 'One Love' armband during the tournament on the threat of receiving a yellow card (three yellow cards equal a red one, which means the player is sent off the field and cannot be replaced). Everybody complied. What role do the personal politics of players play on and off the field?

The format of the tournament was as per usual: public and commercial broadcasters shared matches and offered endless commentary as did online news channels, newspapers and sports magazines. Dedicated talk shows had expert analysis on soccer tactics and strategies, and social media platforms were full of photos and videos of players, fans and everything in between. And yet, the tournament could (have) start(ed) a variety of conversations that go beyond the 'usual' – and that are about much more than 22 men running after a ball...

References

Andréa, Carlos d', and Markus Stauff. 2022. "Mediatized Engagements with Technologies: 'Reviewing' the Video Assistant Referee at the 2018 World Cup." *Communication & Sport* 10 (5): 830–53. https://doi.org/10.1177/21674795221076882.

Bausinger, Hermann. 1984. "Media, Technology and Daily Life." *Media, Culture & Society* 6 (4): 343–51. https://doi.org/10.1177/016344378400600403.

Boyle, Raymond. 2014. "Television Sport in the Age of Screens and Content." *Television & New Media* 15 (8): 746–51. https://doi.org/10.1177/1527476414529167.

Hermes, Joke. 2005. "Burnt Orange: Television, Soccer, and the Representation of Ethnicity." *Television & New Media* 6 (1): 49–69. https://doi.org/10.1177/1527476403255819.

Jorge, Ana, Mercè Oliva, and Luis L.M. Aguiar. 2021. "Offshoring & Leaking: Cristiano Ronaldo's Tax Evasion, and Celebrity in Neoliberal Times." *Popular Communication* 19 (3): 178–92. https://doi.org/10.1080/15405702.2021.1913491.

Kavka, Misha. 2012. *Reality TV*. Edinburgh: University of Edinburgh Press.

O'Connor, Barbara, and Raymond Boyle. 1993. "Dallas with Balls: Televized Sport, Soap Opera and Male and Female Pleasures." *Leisure Studies* 12 (2): 107–19. https://doi.org/10.1080/02614369300390101.

Singh, Sanjesh. 2022. "How Does the World Cup's Viewership, Tickets and Attendance Compare to NFL's Super Bowl? - NBC Sports Bay Area." *NBC Sports*. Accessed March 26, 2023. https://www.nbcsports.com/bayarea/world-cup-2022/how-does-world-cups-viewership-tickets-and-attendance-compare-nfls-super.

Stauff, Markus. 2018. "A Culture of Competition: Sport's Historical Contribution to Datafication." *TMG Journal for Media History* 21 (2): 30. https://doi.org/10.18146/2213-7653.2018.365.

Sterkenburg, Jacco van. 2013. "National Bonding and Meanings Given to Race and Ethnicity: Watching the Soccer World Cup on Dutch TV." *Soccer & Society* 14 (3): 386–403. https://doi.org/10.1080/14660970.2013.801267.

Sterkenburg, Jacco van, Rens Peeters, and Noortje van Amsterdam. 2019. "Everyday Racism and Constructions of Racial/Ethnic Difference in and through Soccer Talk." *European Journal of Cultural Studies* 22 (2): 195–212. https://doi.org/10.1177/1367549418823057.

Whannel, Garry. 2000. "Stars in Whose Eyes?" *Index on Censorship* 29 (4): 48–52. https://doi.org/10.1080/03064220008536760.

13 Visual analysis in practice

Working through, laughing on: pandemic politics, cultural citizenship and action heroes

Method

For this case study, we are combining visual analysis — an exploration of the visual elements of different memes created and shared in the Netherlands during the first months of the Covid-19 pandemic — with a discourse analysis. While other case studies in this book employ either visual analysis or discourse analysis, the combination of these two methods allows for a specific focus on memes and their circulation online.

Research question

The research question for this case study already included a concept right from the start — but one with an open answer: how does the creation and circulation of memes function as a way of 'working through', particularly at moments of crisis?

Data collection

The research question for this chapter comes from a realization of our own practices of sending memes back and forth in a group chat. You might notice that personal habits is how a lot of researchers 'find' the ideas for their new projects — and this is also how you might find ideas for your own projects, papers and assignments. The data collection is also tied to our own practices: In addition to using the memes we sent to each other, we also consciously searched for more memes on the Internet related to the pandemic and asked friends and colleagues for their collections of pandemic memes.

DOI: 10.4324/9781003315421-17

Data analysis

Memes are endlessly recreated images, endlessly traveling, endlessly transforming – collecting and analyzing them at a specific moment in time can give us insights into this specific moment. In our analysis of 'pandemic memes', we found three themes: (1) Working through, (2) Accountability, and (3) Solidarity and Self-Reflexivity. The first one will be the main focus of this chapter. If you are interested in the other themes, have a look at the article we published about pandemic memes (Hermes and Kopitz 2022).

Key concepts

For Cultural citizenship, see Chapter 9

Neoliberalism is a pervasive, increasingly global ideology that believes in competitive markets in all areas of life. It is related to individualism and understands the individual as an entrepreneur whose successes and failures in life are of their own doing. It disavows the existence of unequal power relations and social positions and does not believe in solidarity.

Memes and memefication: Memes are humorous images and animated sequences that spread rapidly on the internet. Users offer variations on a theme and on staple images. Memefication is making something into a meme. Successful memefication means spreading a particular take or comment on the world in a humorous way via the internet, whether critique of the behavior of well-known persons or frustration with ecological threats to the planet or amusement with a cultural phenomenon.

Confronted with the global reality of the Covid-19 pandemic – and its constantly shifting and changing rules and regulations – we all had to find ways to 'work through' an unprecedented moment of crisis. Stanley Tucci started to make cocktails on Instagram. Fitness influencers came up with 'apartment friendly' jumping jack on YouTube. All of us, undoubtedly, worried. This notion of worry – and of channeling worry into something productive – also returned in the media coverage. Especially in the early months of the global pandemic, we praised solidarity and the creative solutions that were pioneered to keep society going: Italians singing from balconies, the British clapping for carers, displays of cardboards in windows as encouragement to your neighbors. A better world we speculated might be the outcome of this crisis. All of these moments, quite crucially, were also shared, circulated and applauded online, crossing the national borders and moving via the internet into the Netherlands – the focus of our research here.

This chapter focuses on our own practices as users and researchers and explores how the creation and circulation of memes functions as another way of 'working through' a crisis. One of our key theoretical concepts for this exploration is cultural citizenship: the multiple ways we connect with each other – and construct our own sense of identity in relationship to others. Or, as Joke Hermes defines it: "cultural citizenship can be found when reconstructing what fuels ongoing conversation and discussion, and how, in and through those exchanges, we connect with others, with places and spaces, with stories and ideas" (2024, 14). Using widely shared memes about the Dutch response to the Covid-19 pandemic in the first half of 2020 as a starting point, we suggest that studying memes as a shared (both figuratively and literally) form of public – pandemic – communication can help us understand cultural citizenship in practice. With that, we are following what Altay, Berriche and Acerbi propose as a counter to one of the common misconceptions about misinformation: "The internet is not rife with misinformation or news, but with memes and entertaining content" (2023, 1). Before you begin to wonder about what memes have to do in a book about television: key televisual images circulate widely, whether scenes from shows, or characters. They return in various shapes and forms. Memes, a key image with a tagline that can be read as a humorous comment, are an example of television 'going places'. And the memes we are discussing in this chapter are also directly or indirectly connected to television news.

Definition: what makes a meme a meme?

As with all media today, memes are globally traveling content. Defined as "(a) group of digital items sharing common characteristics of content, form, and/or stance, which (b) were created with awareness of each other, and (c) were circulated, imitated, and/ or transformed via the Internet by many users" (Shifman 2016, 41), memes are endlessly recreated images, endlessly traveling, endlessly transforming. The most popular memes feature a small number of stock celebrities that are paired with a tagline which renders the image into absurdist reflection on almost every human activity imaginable. From Grumpy Cat, presumed to be one of these first memes, the (expanding) list of 'memeable' faces includes action heroes (predominantly Chuck Norris and Arnold Schwarzenegger), singers such as Drake, the long passed painter Bob Ross and Kermit, the Frog.

Using our own sharing back and forth of toilet paper memes as a starting point, we noticed that pandemic cultural citizenship played out as a vast exercise in disciplining and distinction through jokes and anger – but that there also seemed to be something else hiding underneath the negotiation of the moment. Revolving around toilet paper as a cultural artifact, the memes discussed here are connected not just through their shareability, but the nostalgic thread running through them. Drawing on key images featuring Arnold Schwarzenegger, Kermit the Frog and the Dutch prime minister flanked by Drake, we will ask whether and how the paradox of 'pandemic cultural citizenship' might not have to do especially with Covid. Was this moment of a seemingly unprecedented crisis also a coming to terms with neoliberalism as it has unfolded from the 1980s onwards, and in many ways broke older ideals of solidarity in democratic societies? Are pandemic memes a nostalgic nod to a past that feels 'lost' in the present? The material suggests a nostalgic turn that might point to an implicitly voiced critique of neoliberal governmentality. We are interested in how, on social media and in the spreadable format of memes, humor was used to address and negotiate the public good.

Memes and method: visual analysis in practice

From early on in the pandemic we have collected memes that spoke to us, commended our attention as both users and researchers. Analytically, this growing collection of memes, consisting of over a hundred examples that circulated in the spring of 2020 is approached as embodying a particular type of discursive practice that integrates visual popular culture, comedy and humor in negotiation of a crisis. The dataset is indicative of the trends we observed throughout our networks. Asking others and regularly using open internet search terms (pandemic meme, the specifically Dutch 'hamsteren' or hoarding and terms that developed out of the earlier set) has given our sample a robustness beyond a convenience sample, as 'snowballing' will do (Benneworth 2015, 12).

For the analysis, we brought together a visual analysis of the elements in them – their aesthetics – with a discourse analysis to identify themes and recurring tropes within this ever-growing collection. Such an approach leans on the traditions of semiotic and narrative research (Hawkes 2004): It takes key images and their absurd and incongruous juxtaposition with short texts into account as well as the fact that they are all presented as one via social media. This corresponds to Putzo's understanding of the *material* presentation of texts. Memes, as digital collage, intend to comment and ridicule by means of humor at a single glance (2012, 397). The instantaneity of this 'single glance' is also crucial to our reading of the examples presented here: Contrary to what is customary in semiotics, we are not looking for hidden meaning, but are going with the 'in your face' immediacy of memes. In their obviousness, the memes we saw relied on a friendly humor rather than punishing forms of satire or ridicule, thereby strengthening our interpretation of pandemic meme culture as nostalgic.

Data collection: when is it 'enough'?

Our data for this chapter are memes – recycled and remixed images that are in themselves hard to 'grasp'. The vast magnitude of memes making their way around the world daily makes it virtually impossible to do a 'check' on themes, chart them or produce a representative overview. Of course, social media platforms use their algorithms to tell us what is 'trending', what is currently most popular and what has been shared most widely on a longer timeline. These same algorithms will also isolate users in their 'filter bubbles'. Likely, an impartial overview is altogether illusory. Even if technically achievable, it would not approach users' everyday experience – which is an important aspect of the way memes commend public issues for our attention. From early on in the pandemic, we have collected memes that spoke to us, commended our attention as both users and researchers. This duality is important here – and of course requires you to be self-reflective in your selection.

This smaller study – limited by its national focus and relatively short time frame – might be scaled up in future to do more thoroughly grounded theory building. Yet, while mainly a close reading of a limited dataset, it does connect popular culture to broader themes of citizenship. It allows understanding shared characteristics of meme humor in relation to broader logics of nationalism, citizenship and governmentality that are highly relevant to the field of cultural and media studies. The emphasis in the analysis lies on reconstructing the key arguments presented explicitly and implicitly across the corpus in the collected memes. Thereby, it foregrounds the cultural logic in and of meme use in the Netherlands in the first half of 2020 as a form of public – pandemic – communication.

In the memes posted, shared and commented on in the Netherlands in the first half of 2020, we found three themes: (1) *Working through*, (2) *Accountability* and (3) *Solidarity and Self-Reflexivity* – the first one we will discuss in this chapter as an example of analyzing memes. If you are interested in the other themes, you can find them in an article we published in the *Journal of Media & Cultural Studies Continuum* in 2022. For our discussion of the theme *(1) Working through*, the seeming dominance of the 1980s and their aesthetic is of particular interest to us. The nostalgic joy in revisiting cultural icons of the past is afforded by widely available software on smartphones and meme generators[1] that allows anyone who feels like it to produce one and send it to friends to send on. They are the quintessential 'spreadable media' that Jenkins, Ford and Green (2013, 3) describe as having the potential — both technical and cultural — for audiences to share content for their own purposes, sometimes with the permission of rights holders, sometimes against. We assume in this article that Kermit, Drake and Schwarzenegger (who figures prominently in our analysis below) will be known to international audiences. We do not, however, assume that their visual appearance and names will carry identical meaning. Indeed, part of the strength of meme culture is its local adaptability. Although meme culture like Covid is a global phenomenon, we need to take into account Kuipers' warning that "'world culture' may show considerable national variation" (2015, 987). Wherever necessary we will briefly elucidate intractable uniquely Dutch aspects to the memes discussed below. Clearly, this also implies that we cannot nor do we want to claim that pandemic citizenship works exactly the same elsewhere, even though we hope the Dutch example might prove relatable in other national contexts.

Working through: action heroes and controlling unexpected situations

In the pandemic memes we collected, the global and the local are in an interesting dance. For it was Arnold Schwarzenegger, among others, a global cultural icon who mediated for the Dutch (as for many other language communities) the extreme change of suddenly having to 'stay in place', with a lock-down the answer to the pandemic across many of the countries faced with infection. Memes "sparking of user-created derivatives articulated as parodies, remixes, or mashups" (Shifman 2016, 2) are a productive site to not only acknowledge the challenges faced in an unprecedented situation but also a starting point to work through them. Memes extended the work television does as described by John Ellis, providing "a relatively safe area in which uncertainty can be entertained, and can be entertaining" (2000, 82). 'Working through' is how John Ellis understands (broadcast) television's functioning socially as a collective means to address what we fear and need to come to terms with. Following the global appeal of popular culture and the spreadability of global memes in a national context, the memes were part 'Dutchified', part left with their original texts and contexts. Using 'The Terminator' as a means of coming to terms – pun fully intended – takes on particular significance for an argument about the culmination and continuance of neoliberalist attitudes: Arnold Schwarzenegger as the embodiment of 'the' action hero of the 1980s functions in these memes as a communicative vessel to negotiate questions of individualism and collectivity, of personal needs and the common good.

Humor in the case of this article is at work in two completely different ways. On the one hand, it allows playing with language and social roles, and the mocking of authority (James 2004, 367). On the other hand, it is a collective berating of those represented, and perhaps a means for those laughing to feel united in, as it were, a carnivalesque manner (James 2004; Lockyer and Pickering 2008). Humor, according to Dahl (2021, 45–6), is an "'unserious mode of communication' that can be put to use in the public sphere as unsolvable but productive tension". Humor's ambivalence (Kuipers 2015, 14) would seem to be at the heart of pandemic citizenship, it is neither solely subversion or socialization, as James (2004) suggests for children's literature, but it is both. Specific memes might even be said to link pandemic citizenship to the carnivalesque, reflecting as they do on roles and rules while also rebelling against them (Stallybras and White 1986). Humor on social networks "can be used as a tool of disagreement and protest, (-) to express support and appreciation" (Kráľovičová 2020, 300). Even tasteless and offensive humor can help work through deep crises, as Kuipers (2005, 2002) notes when writing about 9/11 disaster jokes. Not governed by the rules of formal public speech, as in political debate, humor is the means of "the sage fool who can speak truth to power" (Dahl 2021, 49). It allows for boundary work across genres and across social domains and divisions, as well as across media platforms and networks (Dahl 2021; Doona 2021; Kraľovičová 2020).

Humor's play between authority and rebellion is at the heart of the 1980s blockbusters featured and remixed in the memes discussed in this section: As a former 'Black Ops' commando on a personal revenge mission in *Commando* (1985) or as a sometimes-villain-sometimes-hero Cyborg in the *Terminator* franchise, the cinematic action heroes played by Arnold Schwarzenegger throughout the 1980s and 1990s are in any case bordering on the carnivalesque. For instance, a meme remixing the camouflaged and muscled body of Arnold Schwarzenegger's Special Forces Colonel "John Matrix" in *Commando* (1985) now featured a roll of toilet paper instead of the original bazooka on his shoulder. Cropping up again and again in the host of toilet paper memes, the uselessness of sheer muscle and bodily strength against a virus but potential value in an (imaginary) fight in the toilet paper aisle are what intrigues us here.

Arnold Schwarzenegger remained politically active following his time as governor of California. He has been a staunch critic[2] of Donald Trump's pandemic 'strategies' with his, also virally shared, exclamation: "Trust the experts, ignore the morons". Here though he returns in his parade role as muscled action hero in different variations. Playing with the absurdity of both the plot and the aesthetics of the 1980s blockbusters he starred in, these memes can be read as a guide to working through the apparently shifting priorities of pandemic survival. Twisting the official tagline of *Commando* (1985), the first meme[3] plays with Arnie's recognizable star persona as someone willing to do anything for his (personal) cause:

"They hunted him down. They murdered his friends. Now they've taken the one thing he would kill for - his toilet paper. May Heaven help them".

Positioning toilet paper as the one, non-negotiable thing that one would be willing to kill for underlines the changing status of this personal hygiene article. Personal, here, takes on specific importance. Before the spring of 2020, we had not consciously discussed toilet paper with each other, or remembered talking much about toilet paper in general (except the casual random reminder to please buy some). Suddenly, though, toilet paper became an urgent topic of conversation, apparently the one thing to keep us from losing our civility, and a shared cultural artifact to draw on in our shared working through of pandemic politics.

This notion of toilet paper as a the bare necessity for survival is also central to the second example, which uses one of the most famous scenes from Schwarzenegger's *Terminator 2: Judgement Day* (1991): Traveling back in time to 1995, the cyborg protagonist marches into a motorcycle bar in search of clothes (worn by somebody else). Above the film still of Schwarzenegger facing off against one of the gang members in the bar, the original dialogue "I need your clothes, boots…" is added in bold white font. Underneath the film still, however, the dialogue continues differently now. The forcefully requested items – by a naked bodybuilder, no less – in the pandemic version now includes toilet paper instead of the motorcycle he originally demanded. The joke seems to cast the motorcycle's mobility against toilet paper's link to a sedentary life and having to stay not just at home, but to be quartered with your own excrement. As the fight or flight reaction to danger goes, the toilet paper seems to underline the wish to be able to flee by paradoxically focusing on fight. The Schwarzenegger toilet paper memes more directly of course also address the demanding tone and self-serving attitude of pandemic shoppers, whether resulting from panic or privilege. And the rest? May heaven help them. Hoarding toilet paper is, thus, associated with anti-social behavior and a lack of solidarity. Those who do so are accused of misidentifying with the 1980s action hero, those who use the image appear to enjoy a camp moment of nostalgia. Action heroes such as Schwarzenegger were never taken overly seriously, but they were understood as acting for the sake of the common good. That seems exactly what is lost with Covid-19.

Discussion and conclusion: back to the future?

Writing about the first weeks of the pandemic involved a negotiation of our pre- and post-pandemic perspectives, what we understood as humorous then and now and what we think the memes tell us about how the crisis was negotiated. Intriguingly, we found that key images from that first period, reference the 1980s in what looks like a nostalgic turn. In these, the hoarding of toilet paper was a central trope. Why was an illness (not specifically known for causing diarrhea) connected via toilet paper to the end of culture as we knew it? Did the memes show concern over the potential loss of civilization or did they reflect on and ridicule such concerns and should be read as a plea for solidarity against a social code that is all about keeping up appearances, rather than tackling what threatens us collectively? Do they speak to an emergent critique of neoliberalism?

Now officially 'after' the pandemic – at least from a Dutch perspective – we continue to ask ourselves what constitutes responsibility and solidarity – and how we could or should deal with the normalization of the new normal. What was meant to initially be a query of the early weeks of the pandemic in the Netherlands from today's perspective, pointed us toward a much longer timeline. The nostalgic aesthetic and distinct 1980s 'look and feel' of the memes we collected extends to more recent examples. We still see the references to 1980s action films, the sense that neoliberal politics and politicians are overstepping boundaries (the Netherlands meanwhile has also witnessed two major political scandals), the references to the television series *Stranger Things* (both the setting of the series and its visual homage to popular culture of the 1980s) as well as Drake sporting his 'MTV aesthetic'. Using these visuals as a backdrop, the content of the memes discussed here may not be about (pandemic) politics – but political commentary is entangled within them nonetheless.

While our reading of these themes is limited by the sample size and timeframe, it is clear that the references to the 1980s we have noticed serve a nostalgic need for a period of time that preceded the experience of media globalism, neoliberalism and of time losing pre-given rhythms of media and personal communication: of a television schedule, of phoning when you were at home *or* at work but not while on the way in between. The 1980s are 'just' before the breakthrough of commercial television in the Netherlands (from 1990 onwards), 'just' before the spread of mobile telecommunications in the early 1990s and 'just' before neoliberalism was fully embraced across the political spectrum by the late 1990s. The re-emergence of the 1980s, at least visually, points to the conclusion that Covid memes may not offer a forum for political discussion. But that they are, indeed, a 'coming to terms' with the pandemic as a wake-up call to the economic and social logic of localized global neoliberalism. However, ambivalent a reaction they may be to the pandemic, the memes discussed here can be read as a highly meaningful form of 'pandemic' cultural citizenship. Humor and satire connect the like-minded (Tesnohlidkova 2020, 9), and so do memes in their ever-shifting usage of both. They provide a sense of belonging and a forum for implicit discussion of public issues for people who are not likely to ever meet. They offer laughter to work through the burden of pandemic society. To quote @nickcaveandthebadmemes: 'Damn it, funny internet people! I'm trying to let out the sad!'

More memes? Reading recommendation: *Critical Meme Reader* edited by Chloé Arkenbout and Laurence Scherz (2022)

Already in its second edition, the Critical Meme Reader features work by researchers, activists and artists on memes and their relation to questions of politics and power, individual practices and shared meanings, pasts and futures.

Notes

1 For instance, see https://www.kapwing.com/meme-maker.
2 Arnold on Twitter: "Stay at home as much as possible. Listen to the experts, ignore the morons (foreheads). We will get through this together.... https://t.co/YkUiQbDkRT"
3 Considering the spreadable logic and 'mashed-up' character of memes, providing an original source is somewhat impossible. Instead, we are pointing towards the first recognised source for each meme while acknowledging that their idea might have originated somewhere else.

References

Altay, Sacha, Manon Berriche, and Alberto Acerbi. 2023. "Misinformation on Misinformation: Conceptual and Methodological Challenges." *Social Media + Society* 9 (1): 205630512211504. https://doi.org/10.1177/20563051221150412.
Arkenbout, Chloë, and Laurence Scherz (Eds). 2022. *Critical Meme Reader II. Memetic Tacticality*. Amsterdam: Institute of Network Cultures.

Benneworth, Paul. 2015. "Between Certainty and Comprehensiveness in Evaluating the Societal Impact of Humanities Research." CHEPS Working Papers 02/15.

Dahl, John. 2021 "Voices on the Border. Comedy and Immigration in the Scandinavian Public Spheres." PhD thesis U of Bergen.

Doona, Joanna. 2021. "News Satire Engagement as a Transgressive Space for Genre Work." *International Journal of Cultural Studies* 24 (1): 15–33. https://doi.org/10.1177/1367877919892279.

Ellis, John. 2000. *Seeing Things: Television in the Age of Uncertainty.* London/New York: I.B. Tauris.

Hawkes, Terence. 2004. *Structuralism and Semiotics.* 2nd ed. London: Routledge.

Hermes, Joke. 2024. *Cultural Citizenship and Popular Culture. The Art of Listening.* London: Routledge.

Hermes, Joke, and Linda Kopitz. 2022. "'We Can Sh*t for Another 10 Years.' Toilet Paper, Pandemic Politics and Cultural Citizenship." *Continuum* 36 (2): 244–59. https://doi.org/10.1080/10304312.2021.1998373.

James, Kathryn. 2004. "Subversion or Socialization? Humor and Carnival in Morris Gleitzman's Texts." *Childrens Literature in Education* 35 (4): 367–79. https://doi.org/10.1007/s10583-004-6418-x.

Jenkins, Henry, Sam Ford, and Joshua Green. 2013. *Spreadable Media. Creating Value and Meaning in a Networked Media.* New York, NY: NYU Press.

Kraľovičová, Denisa. 2020. "Humour and Social Networks during COVID-19." *Marketing Identity* 1: 300–7.

Kuipers, Giselinde. 2002. "Media Culture and Internet Disaster Jokes: Bin Laden and the Attack on the World Trade Center." *European Journal of Cultural Studies* 5 (4): 450–70. https://doi.org/10.1177/1364942002005004296.

———. 2005. "'Where Was King Kong When We Needed Him?' Public Discourse, Digital Disaster Jokes, and the Functions of Laughter after 9/11." *The Journal of American Culture* 28 (1): 70–84. https://doi.org/10.1111/j.1542-734X.2005.00155.x.

———. 2015. *Good Humor, Bad Taste: A Sociology of the Joke.* Berlin: Walter de Gruyter GmbH & Co KG.

Lockyer, Sharon, and Michael Pickering. 2008. "You Must Be Joking: The Sociological Critique of Humour and Comic Media: Humour and Comic Media." *Sociology Compass* 2 (3): 808–20. https://doi.org/10.1111/j.1751-9020.2008.00108.x.

Putzo, Christine. 2012. "The Implied Book and the Narrative Text: On a Blind Spot in Narratological Theory – from a Media Studies Perspective." *Journal of Literary Theory* 6 (2). https://doi.org/10.1515/jlt-2012-0004.

Shifman, Limor. 2016. "Cross-Cultural Comparisons of User-Generated Content: An Analytical Framework." *International Journal of Communication* 10: 5644–63.

Stallybrass, Peter, and Allon White. 1986. *The Politics and Poetics of Transgression.* Ithaca: Cornell University Press.

Tesnohlidkova, Olivera. 2020. "Humor and Satire in Politics: Introducing Cultural Sociology to the Field." *Sociology Compass* 15.1 (2021): e12842.

14 The long interview in practice

Looking back: remembering favorite teen television shows

WITH ERINN RÖVEKAMP

Method

For audience researchers, returning to the past can be a great opportunity for new insights. The chapter draws on seven long, qualitative, open interviews Erinn held with friends for her research master's thesis. The respondents of this case study all love television and having a good chat about it. Asking friends to be her respondents allowed Erinn to create an interview situation with no pressure – an environment where it is easy to open up and reflect on personal memories.

Research question

Interested in body diversity, Erinn used her own memories as a starting point to explore the tension between nostalgic memories and critical distance. How did her respondents remember the television shows of way back when? Did they happen to have a sense of how teen and teenage bodies are represented in series for young viewers?

Data collection

Here is how the initial research project was set up: Erinn started auto-ethnographically and reflected on her own experiences and favorite childhood series. Noticing a discrepancy between her memories and what the shows looked like when she watched them again, she decided to interview friends about their childhood television favorites. All interviews were recorded and transcribed in full. To finish the project, she contacted her informants again and checked for validity (did she get it right)? This way,

DOI: 10.4324/9781003315421-18

she also made good on her earlier ethical commitment to not publish any statements or descriptions that might make her friends recognizable or that would represent them in hurtful ways. The names used for the informants/co-researchers are pseudonyms.

Data analysis

From an adult perspective, It turned out that sizeism and racism are easy enough to spot in tween and teen television shows (when you start looking for it), but, apparently, they are hard to recognize when you are just being a viewer enjoying yourself. Erinn analyzed the interview transcripts using a discourse analysis method developed by Jonathan Potter and Margaret Wetherell (1988). The interviews were coded to select statements about the representation of bodies in teen television. The open codes were then clustered into axial codes which allowed for the final step, which is selective coding (Strauss and Corbin 1990). It resulted in several themes, such as the different exigencies for female and male characters, the exclusion of bigger bodies, nostalgic pleasure and the difference between Dutch teen television and teen programs made elsewhere. Selective coding, the third step, showed how informants became aware of the normalizing power of visual regimes. Time for Erinn, as the central researcher, to check back with the literature about teen television (of which there is a lot), fat-shaming and nostalgia. Using the interviews as a guide, Erinn then analyzed the undisputed top 13 shows (that were mentioned in all the interviews) to analyze these for their representation of bodies using intersectional visual analysis.

Key concepts

A *visual regime* is a set of rules that governs how, e.g., bodies are to be shown in film and television. An example of such a rule system is that bodies need to be 'fit' and slender rather than big and flabby. When bodies do not comply with this rule, this is meaningful and needs explanation. Nonconformity tells us something about a character or a person.

Nostalgia is to long for a period from the past that is made out to be more positive and pleasant than it was. *Memory* is recollection and while often faulty, it is not understood as intentional misrepresentation.

Representation: description or portrayal as in 'making present again'. Representation is an act that produces a new situation or image as it references persons or events. See Chapter 2.

From *Pokémon* to *Totally Spies* to *The Suite Life of Zack and Cody*: do you also remember these television shows? Even though memories are far from reliable,[1] asking others about their memories of the television of their youth provides a wonderful point of entry. The ensuing conversation might be about being a teen, teen television or television itself of course. Talking about television memories can turn to social issues. In this chapter, that issue is body diversity – of which there seems to be remarkably little in teen television. As with other examples in this book, the 'spark' for this project was a personal one. Talking to friends about what they remembered about television way back when, Erinn realized that her head was filled with slim-bodied, slender-legged girls to whom it had felt really difficult to measure up. For her research master's thesis in television studies, Erinn wanted to return to teen and tween television and explore how once beloved shows are difficult to rewatch.

What teen television series do you remember?

The participants interviewed for this project listed 13 series as their teen 'favorites': *Drake & Josh* (Nickelodeon, 2004–2007), *Glee* (Fox, 2009–2015), *Het Huis Anubis* (Studio 100, 2006–2009), *iCarly* (Nickelodeon, 2007–2012), *Ned's Declassified School Survival Guide* (Nickelodeon, 2004–2007), *Pokémon* (Nintendo, 1997-present), *Rocket Power* (Nickelodeon, 1999–2004), *Spangas* (KRO-NCRV, 2007-present), *That's So Raven* (Disney Channel, 2003–2007), *The Suite Life of Zack and Cody* (Disney Channel, 2005–2008), *Totally Spies* (Cartoon Network, 2001–2013), *Winx Club* (Nickelodeon, 2004-present) and *ZOOP* (Dutch Nickelodeon, 2004–2007). Most of these shows appeared on all seven informants' lists.

The key methodology this chapter speaks to is the classic long interview: These are interviews that will last upward of an hour and a half. Rather than questions, the interviewer uses a topic list or prompts such as a set of images. Here, the respondents were a group of friends who all love television. Their querying of teen television shows brings together audience-led analysis and ethnographic methods. The seven interviews were open conversations without any pressure to be critical. Erinn used prompts and had her informants go back to the shows they had loved most – with a specific focus on the body types of main characters. Simply looking at images of the characters in those old shows almost immediately made the real lack of diversity obvious. Anyone taking a look at teen television will be able to observe that youth actors and animated figures are predominantly slender and able-bodied. Yet, when remembering the television you used to love (without actually seeing a program again), it seems you do not have the critical distance to see this. As if the slim 'televisual' body is such a 'normal' thing, that it is really hard to recognize that something is amiss.

From feeling nostalgic to feeling ... uneasy?

Remembered television feels 'true'. However media literate and critical we become as grown-ups, we retain a soft spot for the series we saw when young. In a sense then, they have shaped how we perceive the world. Most of us do not go back to those early series. It will be by chance that you become aware of the limitations in how, in this case, teen television represents body types, ethnicity, ability or sexuality. Erinn and her friends all felt deeply betrayed when they rewatched the series that were produced for them when they were tweens and teens. Returning to them now, with a bit of distance, revealed insidious forms of exclusion and stereotyping. The interviews all started on a positive note. 'Love' was a term used often to describe the feelings that surfaced when discussing favorite shows. This was the opening 'exercise' of the interview.

> *Oh my god, I loved, I loved it.* - Jente

Suddenly, remembering a particular series or a character was thrilling and 'brought back memories'. This initial enthusiasm would then shift toward a feeling of discomfort when Erinn asked about the representation of bodies in the series.

> *It shouldn't be something that we should be noticing!* - Chloé
> *That's intense, now that I look at it!* - Coco
> *But why would they lie about this so much?* - Theodorus

Discomfort is expressed here in different ways. Chloé was deeply annoyed when she realized that overweight characters are underrepresented and portrayed negatively. We should not be able to notice the difference in representation between slim and overweight characters because there should not *be* a difference in the first place, she argued. Coco was shocked. She uses the word 'now' to suggest that she had not realized to what extent body types are misrepresented before and found it very 'intense'. Lastly, Theodorus felt betrayed. Why did the show he loved so much as a kid now seem to be based on problematic representations of bodies? The quotes show how general feelings toward teen television changed from happy and nostalgic to annoyed and uneasy as these television viewers started to recognize the limited frame of reference of body representation used throughout popular youth series made in the early 2000s. Analyzing the material, three overarching themes surfaced.

Theme 1: lack of body diversity

The first of the themes is *lack of body diversity*. It did not take Erinn and her friends long to recognize something was amiss in the representation of bodies:

> *Yeah [the characters] were all quite similar, and the only thing that would set them apart would be their clothing and their hairstyle.* - Chloé

> *I think there is in general something to say about everybody being skinny and that there wasn't as much body diversity on television. (…) I would say that all the main characters were all skinny.* - Stormy

> *I can't even remember if there's a show with a fat girl in there. Is there?* - Jente

> *There are no fat kids.* - Sterre

A double argument is constructed here. On the one hand, the similarity of the bodies of characters is striking. On the other hand, characters are visually differentiated through details such as the color of their hair or the way they dress. Stormy recognizes that there is a preference for thin bodies: all main characters were 'skinny'. Checking these observations against the research literature, there is unambiguous support that television has a preference for the slim-bodied.[2] Network television programming has an overall preference for "young and thin" main characters, according to Sylvia White and her colleagues (1999). Other studies show how there is, indeed, an unequal division of body sizes. Thin characters are overrepresented in comparison to overweight characters, say Bradley Greenberg and his colleagues (2003) as well as others. Beauty ideals on the *Disney* and *Nickelodeon* channels are no different: the thin ideal also dominates series for younger viewers (Northup and Liebler 2010).

Lack of diversity is underlined by the different ways in which girls and boys' bodies are depicted. Erinn and friends started noticing that all the girl characters had hourglass figures:

> *(Girls' bodies are) very much exaggerated and sexualized as well, because of the outfit. But also the whole body, of course it's big boobs, small waist, big ass and tall legs. And you know, the whole sort of Barbie-like thing, of course.* - Coco

Coco makes an interesting argument here, as she notes how unrealistic the representation of female bodies is, their bodies are 'exaggerated' she says – and not just on television. However physically impossible, Barbie is understood to embody Western female beauty standards (Rice et al. 2016, 142). Coco also notes that girls' bodies are sexualized. She later explains:

> *And you know, now looking at them, they were also very exposed. They always wore clothes until like, up till there [pointing towards her midriff]. And then it was just naked. That's interesting.* - Coco

Other informants also touched upon the sexualization of female characters:

> *Yes, they were really portrayed as sexual objects.* - Jente

> *Sex symbol, you know, blonde hair, boobs and then she's like, she is a little bit typical.* - Samuel (he talks about *Totally Spies*)

Visual analysis works well when picking up on these observations. The sexualization of young female bodies is everywhere. Whether in *Totally Spies*, *Winx Club* or *Pokémon*. The hourglass figure of the three girls in *Totally Spies*, for instance, is emphasized through their (lack of) clothing. In the opening sequence, for example, Sam, Clover and Alex are standing in the hallway of their high school, with lockers on the right side of the screen and other pupils in the background. Sam wears a fitting blue dress that 'hugs' her figure. It shows off her smaller waist and larger hips. Her cleavage is emphasized by a collar that opens into a deep cut. The dress ends above the knee. Combined with matching white-and-blue heels, her long slim legs are shown off. Clover is wearing red heels, tight pink pants and a matching red blouse. It is open at the bottom and reveals part of her belly. Similar to Sam, Clover also has an open collar which brings attention to her cleavage. As Clover's blouse is only closed in the middle, it emphasizes her small waist. The way the blouse flows open at the bottom in addition creates the illusion of bigger hips. Dark-haired Alex is wearing green knee-high boots, a pink shirt and a matching green crop top with spaghetti straps, also revealing her belly. It is her tight and revealing crop top that brings attention to her hourglass figure. All episodes of the first season have these revealing, feminine outfits.

The camera framing and the opening shot in the leader make it even worse. It is a tilt up from the feet to the head. We see three pairs of long legs walking in a school hallway toward the camera, in which the camera tilts up to show the rest of the girls' bodies. It literally checks the girls out. Not only are the three girls displayed sexually, we are also explicitly invited to look at them that way. This goes back to a long discussion in cinema studies and visual analysis. Film scholar Laura Mulvey, famously, spoke of how mainstream film (and television) invites a 'male gaze' (1975). Nicholas Mirzoeff (2011) adds that cinematic technology (the law of the gaze) will suddenly become 'the right to look'. As a result, the girls' bodies are now infused with sexuality. They may well dress to suit their own tastes. The camera does not care and recasts them as presented for our pleasure.

There is a second, even more insidious effect of the sexualized female body in a teen cartoon series. Not only are we socialized into thinking that women's bodies are there to be enjoyed (regardless of what the person in the body thinks or wants), their body shape tends to completely take over the characters' identities as well. In *Totally Spies*, the girls' identities are built around their appearance. They frequently discuss how they look (and how others will see them):

> *Wait, I can't go! I left my new sunglasses at home.* (Episode 5, 00:04:55)

> *Fashion crisis! I need to pick out what to wear on my date. [...] Number one rule in dating: the outfit is everything! Wait, isn't that the number one rule in life?* (Episode 12, 00:04:24)

> *But Sammy would never miss out on our ritual Thursday night shopping spree.* (Episode 19, 00:08:40)

Even when the girls are out on a dangerous mission, they complain about the 'costumes' they need to wear for their undercover role, or the way that their mission ruins their clothing, hair or make-up:

> *We're almost in the lava and this heat is ruining my hair!* (Episode 4, 00:15:24)

> *Jerry! You know what stress does to my skin!* (Episode 14, 00:02:33)

> *A good swim will tone our calves.* (Episode 15, 00:06:18)

> *My lips are seriously chapped.* (Episode 21, 00:16:11)

As viewers, we are constantly reminded that your appearance is crucial to your identity as a woman. The plots emphasize this too. Clover overeating on cookies in episode 21 of season 1 is a good example. Not only is it usually Clover, the blonde one, who gets into trouble (a stereotypical association of hair with intelligence), she also becomes monstrous when the cookie overeating makes her severely overweight. She is blond and silly and fat, and no longer attractive. Plotlines tend to combine the girls' appearances, whether their outfits or hair, with wanting to impress a boy. The series is instructing its viewers on what is important to a young woman:

Having television shows routinely stress the importance of dating could serve to reinforce the notion that in order to be popular, one needs to have a boyfriend, and in order to get a boyfriend, one needs to be thin and attractive. This message can also be seen as part of the increasing sexualization that is occurring to young females in the media today.

(Northup and Liebler 2010, 271)

It does not matter that much of this attention to the body is humorous and made into a joke. The attention paid to the ideal of the slim body and to looking good and, therefore, being attractive to men in order to be successful as a (young) woman, is relentless.

Theme II: the 'funny' overweight white boy

The second theme to emerge is body negativity. Not only are thin bodies the norm, there is also a dearth of overweight bodies. The few well-rounded characters appear to HAVE to have very specific characteristics in addition. These could be positive, such as having a sense of humor:

the only shows where someone would be heavy, they would be portrayed as like the funny guy I think - Chloé

Yeah, the fat guy is the funny guy. - Jente

When Chloe and Jente refer to 'the funny guy', they note that overweight *male* characters are portrayed differently than overweight female characters. Are 'funny guys', a character with a sense of humor or a character who viewers can laugh at, Stormy wondered:

There is a very big distinction between being the funny guy and being made fun of. (…) I think when they talk about fatter characters in the storyline where that's of interest, it's making fun of. - Stormy

Stormy uses a character from *Glee* as an example. Mercedes starts a riot when the school cafeteria decides to stop selling 'tater tots'. Tater tots are grated, deep-fried potatoes formed into small blocks that are eaten as a snack or as a side dish. It does not make the full-bodied Mercedes into a funny character. The opposite is the case. Viewers are invited to laugh *at* her. Jente agreed: there is a big difference between a character being funny and being made fun of:

And the butt of the joke is the fat guy. - Jente

Once they are 'on' to how overweight characters carry a particular burden of representing what is socially undesirable, Erinn and friends realized these characters tend to be 'clumsy' and 'lonely' and that they 'do not get girlfriends'. Clearly, in the universe constructed by and through these series, it cannot be much fun to be fat.

Suggestions for further reading about the representation of bodies on television

Television drama portrays thin bodies in a positive light, whereas overweight characters are predominantly represented in a negative light. Thin characters more often than not embody desirable character traits in their television persona, such as being attractive, kind and happy (Greenberg et al. 2003, 1342; Himes and Thompson 2007, 713). Overweight characters, on the other hand, are often "ridiculed and shown to be undesirable in a variety of ways" (Greenberg et al. 2003, 1342, 1344). They are depicted as unattractive, mean and evil (Himes and Thompson 2007, 713). This constant denigration of overweight characters on television could lead to what has been called "fat stigmatization", which is "the devaluing of an individual due to excess body weight" in real life (Himes and Thompson 2007, 712). Research on series for young viewers argues that children's television shows incorporate and reinforce this stereotype of "beauty is good." Characters that are considered beautiful are the ones that have the desirable character traits (Northup and Liebler 2010, 268). A 'lack' of beauty is associated with negative character traits (Northup and Liebler 2010; Robinson, Calllister and Jankoski 2008).

The negative visual regime of attractive slim women and unappealing overweight guys, can be found in many series (in *Drake & Josh*, *iCarly* and *Rocket Power*, for example, all series that were remembered fondly). Visual analysis again works well to deepen observations from the conversational interviews. *Drake & Josh*, for example, is a series about two teenage step brothers who are each other's complete opposites. They are forced to share a room when their parents get married and move in together. Drake is the handsome, popular guy who gets all the attention of girls, whereas Josh is nerdy, unpopular and socially awkward.

Josh is immediately established as an undesirable character. Within the first five minutes of the show, he is described by Drake as both "unusual" (Episode 1, 00:01:10), "goofy" and "clammy" (Episode 1, 00:04:29), all negative character traits. Josh dresses up as 'Miss Nancy', a character which he designed in order to give advice to people at school anonymously. As Miss Nancy, Josh wears a wig, a colorful flower dress and puts on fake breasts. Drake ridicules him for dressing like a woman and laughs in his face. Josh thus becomes an "object of humor" (Greenberg et al. 2003, 1347). Josh continues to be ridiculed by the other main characters. He confirms his own social awkwardness with girls when he says "It's like me and girls speak different languages. They speak English, I speak idiot" (Episode 5, 00:00:32). Josh is a nerd, a loser who viewers can laugh about and at. The same logic applies to other white male overweight characters, such as Gibby in *iCarly*: They are used for comic relief.

Theme III: the angry black girl

Lastly, a third shared theme suggests that the overweight body is not only a different burden for boys and girls, but especially for black women – whether young or old. Intersections of weight, gender, class and race matter. As will become clear, stereotyping of heavy (young) black women is especially nasty.

> *It was all white people are skinny, and black people are fat.* - Stormy
>
> *They are being framed as in, the black fat person* - Sterre
>
> *Why are white people never fat?* - Chloé

Black characters were often the overweight characters in the 13 series that were discussed. The white female characters on the contrary were always skinny. Chloé noticed how Avalanche, an overweight black female character in the Dutch series *Spangas* is fully defined by her body:

> *You had lots of shows with groups of friends, or groups of characters (…). Mostly white characters. All of them, with the exception of Avalanche, were thin. (…) Well her size was part of the story, as in, yeah I did look it up, but I do remember it now as well, that she was very dominant* - Chloé

Avalanche is a dominant person. The obvious link is to the stereotype of 'the Angry Black Woman'. It suggests big black women are generally "out of control, disagreeable, overly aggressive, physically threatening, loud (even when [speaking] softly), and to be feared" (Jones and Norwoord 2017, 2049). Avalanche fits this mold perfectly. "She had a sharp tongue", says Chloe, and "not really a soft side".

The reason why Avalanche would be heavier has more to do with the fact that she would portray umm, like the angry black woman and powerful black woman, than anything else I think. - Chloé

Not only, apparently, does body size define a character's personality, but, in a perfectly circular logic, black characters are negatively portrayed because they are often the only overweight ones. Visual analysis confirms this for *Glee*, a musical comedy-drama series about a group of teenagers who will form a high school show choir. Five teenagers, who are all represented as outcasts, audition. We are introduced to a boy in a wheelchair, a girl who stutters, two teenagers who are bullied by other students at school, and Mercedes, who is an overweight black girl.

Mixing different forms of analysis for maximum effect in a short essay

By talking about their memories of teen television programs, Erinn and her friends became conscious of the way in which body sizes are evaluated morally and socially. Analysis of their conversation shows how viewers switch between different frames of reference. Those can also be called stories or 'interpretative repertoires'. Both terms relate to *discourse analysis*. Discourse analysis shows how different frames (or repertoires or stories) are a shared 'commodity' in everyday meaning making. Shared cultural systems of reference do not start with individuals, they precede us. By talking we use them and this will change them (because of slightly new forms of use or mistakes or because of cultural and political activism.

Long interviews or collective forms of *auto-ethnography* become more valuable when read through the lens of discourse analysis. It will bring out precisely what is shared and allow for ideological criticism. A researcher interested in identity could also look at Erinn's material *intersectionally*. In that case, the analysis focuses on how cultural frames play out differently at different identity crossroads. Social power relations then become an explicit part of the mix. It allowed Erinn to recognize the moral evaluation of body shape and weight. These are often related to the class position of a character or their race. For more on intersectionality, see Hill Collins and Bilge (2020).

Mercedes is angry. When Mercedes speaks in front of the rest of the Glee club for the first time, she immediately disagrees with the teacher that she is not the lead singer of the group: "OH HELL TO THE NO! I am not down for this background singing nonsense!" (Episode 1, 00:23:54). In episode 16 called 'Home', Mercedes needs to lose ten pounds in order to stay on the cheerleading team (episode 16, 00:01:14). Her friends from Glee club try to tell her she should not feel embarrassed by her body and that she is fine as she is. This kind of compliment, however, confirms that she is overweight, her difference is underlined. Mercedes wants to lose weight though: "To look fantastic. To finally fit into this school". (episode 16, 00:26:03). The message appears to be: Being overweight will make you feel unattractive and undesirable.

Conclusion

Cross-referencing a series of long interviews allows audience researchers to map shared cultural knowledge. Here, that map shows how teen television uses ridiculously simple schemes. Those schemes, moreover, reinforce a series of stereotypes to do with body size, skin and hair color and gender. Focusing a series of interviews on television memories is useful too. It feeds media literacy. Looking back, interviewees come to recognize logics they had not been aware of. As Erinn's example shows, using prompts, images or a quiz can be helpful. When calibrated well (not too difficult or too easy), they will make participants feel comfortable and activate their memories. Once in 'playful' mode, the interview can challenge informants to take a step further and become co-interpreters of the television material that is discussed. While there is always a risk of groupthink and socially desirable answers, the long interview can turn into a form of participative or collaborative autoethnography.

Notes

1 See for example Gardner (2001).
2 See for instance Fouts and Burggraf (1999), Greenberg et al. (2003), White et al. (1999).

References

Fouts, Gregory, and Kimberley Burggraf. 1999. "Television Situation Comedies: Female Body Images and Verbal Reinforcements." *Sex Roles: A Journal of Research* 40 (5/6): 473–81. https://doi.org/10.1023/A:1018875711082.
Gardner, Graham. 2001. "Unreliable Memories and Other Contingencies: Problems with Biographical Knowledge." *Qualitative Research* 1 (2): 185–204. https://doi.org/10.1177/146879410100100205.

Greenberg, Bradley S., Matthew Eastin, Linda Hofschire, Ken Lachlan, and Kelly D. Brownell. 2003. "Portrayals of Overweight and Obese Individuals on Commercial Television." *American Journal of Public Health* 93 (8): 1342–48. https://doi.org/10.2105/AJPH.93.8.1342.

Hill Collins, Patricia, and Sirma Bilge. 2020. *Intersectionality.* 2nd ed. Key Concepts. Cambridge/Medford, MA: Polity Press.

Himes, Susan M., and J. Kevin Thompson. 2007. "Fat Stigmatization in Television Shows and Movies: A Content Analysis." *Obesity*15 (3): 712–18. https://doi.org/10.1038/oby.2007.635.

Jones, Trina, and Kimberly Jade Norwood. 2017. "Aggressive Encounters & White Fragility: Deconstructing the Trope of the Angry Black Woman." *Iowa Law Review*, 2017-69.

Mirzoeff, Nicholas. 2011. *The Right to Look: A Counterhistory of Visuality.* Durham, NC: Duke University Press.

Mulvey, L. 1975. "Visual Pleasure and Narrative Cinema." *Screen* 16 (3): 6–18. https://doi.org/10.1093/screen/16.3.6.

Northup, Temple, and Carol M. Liebler. 2010. "The Good, the Bad, and the Beautiful: Beauty Ideals on the Disney and Nickelodeon Channels." *Journal of Children and Media* 4 (3): 265–82. https://doi.org/10.1080/17482798.2010.496917.

Potter, John, and Margaret Wetherell. 1988. "Discourse Analysis and the Identification of Interpretative Repertoires." In *Analysing Everyday Explanation: A Casebook of Methods*, C. Antaki (Ed.), 168–83. London: Sage Publications.

Rice, Karlie, Ivanka Prichard, Marika Tiggemann, and Amy Slater. 2016. "Exposure to Barbie: Effects on Thin-Ideal Internalisation, Body Esteem, and Body Dissatisfaction among Young Girls." *Body Image* 19 (December): 142–49. https://doi.org/10.1016/j.bodyim.2016.09.005.

Robinson, Tom, Mark Callister, and Tahlea Jankoski. 2008. "Portrayal of Body Weight on Children's Television Sitcoms: A Content Analysis." *Body Image* 5 (2): 141–51. https://doi.org/10.1016/j.bodyim.2007.11.004.

Strauss, Anselm Leonard, and Juliet M. Corbin. 1990. *Basics of Qualitative Research: Grounded Theory Procedures and Techniques.* Newbury Park, CA: Sage Publications.

White, Sylvia E., N. J. Brown, and Sandra L. Ginsburg. 1999. "Diversity of Body Types in Network Television Programming: A Content Analysis." *Communication Research Reports* 16 (4): 386–92. https://doi.org/10.1080/08824099909388740.

15 Afterthought
What's next?

You might think that 14 chapters are plenty of room to introduce the theory and practice of qualitative audience research. But, it turns out that we would not mind going on a bit further – which is what this additional 'Afterthought' is now doing!

To keep this pocketbook accessible and concise, we have not included much of the academic jargon and social-science-lingo that includes terms such as representativity, reliability and generalisability. Here and there they surface. We recommend that, in addition to this book, you take a look at a classic qualitative data analysis handbook. Rather than simply sticking with a quick online search to find definitions, such handbooks give you a sense of the enormous and, in many ways, exciting field that research methodology is. Maybe you enjoy the challenge of reverse-engineering research outcomes – for which active knowledge of methodology is indispensable. **We hope that this book is the catalyst that challenges you to test new methods, or return to 'old' methods with new questions.**

This also links back to the platforms, services and social media examples we draw on in this pocketbook. Looking at the 14 chapters, it is clear that we have often used what audiences had to say about Netflix productions (rather than other services) for no other reason than that it provided us with globally accessible examples. Today, we find ourselves using a much wider range of video and television platform services but have not yet had time to (find) research (about) them in extensive detail. They will have to wait for a next book. Also, the social media that are referenced throughout the book are the set that we have been on the last couple of years. **We hope that you find new and innovative ways to explore audiences and audience practices in, on and through these platforms as well as ones that are bound to come into being before long.**

To show you how we make sense of and find meaning in and through different media, our case studies bring together fans of Turkish soap operas and nostalgic memories of Dutch children's television, soccer fans and viewers watching YouTubers watch a Regency romance. Of course,

DOI: 10.4324/9781003315421-19

we would have loved to include even more audience communities – from gamers and anime fans to classical music aficionados. Maybe your work as an audience researcher can begin where this pocketbook ends. **We hope that you feel encouraged to explore more audiences, fandoms, communities – and reflect on your own position as a viewer-user-fan-and-researcher.**

This 'positionality' also connects to our own practice as audience researchers. Researcher reflexivity is encouraged in audience research. To draw on your own experiences to explore larger questions of representation, belonging and identity is more than helpful. We too engage with media objects that spoke to us – in the best or in the worst way. We explore communities that we are part of, or use our own not-being-part-of as a reason to listen even more carefully. In this pocketbook, the examples we present draw on the balance this requires in recognizing boundaries and connections. Likewise, dealing with painful topics in interviews is important, as is researching what people say and think who hold diametrically opposed views to your own. We have not offered such examples, but they exist and are easy enough to find via university libraries and Google Scholar. One starting point we recommend is Ellen Seiter's seminal 1990 example of 'a troubling interview'. While Seiter addresses her unease, other researchers choose to let their informants speak and frame their views directly. **We hope that you will take the methodological tools presented in this book to venture into the fields and topic areas that speak to you – in a caring and self-reflexive way.**

To emphasize that audience research is much more than 'just' a method, the individual methodology chapters are connected through the larger theme of meaning-making as a shared practice. Although often thought of as specific to media studies, we think that audience research is a transferable skill. Even if you are not going to be a researcher or practitioner in media studies, production, sociology or anthropology: the methods introduced in this pocketbook are skills that are not limited in their uses and usability to a particular field of practice. Audience research includes being able to listen. It includes challenging yourself to understand what you 'hear', including your own interpretative steps and intuitive leaps. **We hope that this resonates as you come up with your own links and connections – in your research within and beyond the university.**

What we hope for most, though, is that you take this pocketbook and the ideas and tools it offers and make them your own. In a range of professional fields, forms of audience research will help you get feedback on your work, or check whether your mediation or management attempts are going well. In all aspects of your life, people will be happy to have someone listen to them – especially someone who knows that paying attention pays, who knows that unequal power relations matter, someone who recognizes that we are both rational and emotional beings. In your research, audience research allows you to explore how we make meaning but also how audiences are placemakers, materially and virtually. As shared practices, in shared spaces and via shared references, they offer crucial elements for belonging. Paying attention to these, academically, professionally, culturally, socially, can contribute to making our universities, our cities, our world a place where more people can feel like they belong.

P.S. Do let us know about your research and what you think of the book!

Index

actuality 96, 98
addiction 22
affect 26, 62, 78, 82, 126, 154;
    affective economy 26
affordance (technological) 13, 23,
    74, 123
agency 20, 23, 30, 83, 126
algorithm 74, 84, 122, 168
analysis: audience-led analysis 4, 14,
    30, 64–76, 177; data analysis
    119–30; discourse analysis
    55–8, 105–18, 141–51,
    164–74, 185; media discourse
    analysis 38, 56–8, 141–51;
    narrative analysis 77; semiotic
    analysis 20, 35, 167; thematic
    analysis 86, 106, 116;
    visual analysis 68, 77–89,
    164–74, 180
appearance 47f, 81f, 120, 181
attention 50, 159, 167
attraction 105–18
audience 3, 11; audience attachments
    78; audiencehood 3, 11
audience-led analysis see analysis
authenticity 54f
authority 79, 91, 126, 138, 139, 170
autoethnography 13, 30, 38, 55–8,
    141, 157, 159; collaborative
    autoethnography 38f, 55–8,
    131–40, 186
autonomy 20, 21

belonging 15, 26, 65, 84, 120, 125,
    144–9, 152, 155, 173, 189f
boundary 43, 112, 170
broadcast 7–11, 70, 92, 154f, 169

casting 38f, 53, 121, 125
citizenship 15, 26, 63, 64, 96; cultural
    citizenship 8, 15, 26, 41, 62f,
    79, 92, 119–30, 166–73
class 9, 19, 63, 72, 84, 124,
    126, 129
clustering 28, 42, 94, 129
codes: axial codes 28f, 37, 44–9, 176;
    open codes 28f, 37, 44–9, 94,
    176; selective codes 28f, 37,
    43, 44–9, 156, 176
coding 28f, 37, 44–9
commercialization 137, 157
commodification 28
community 9, 23, 28, 60–2, 64–6,
    72, 111, 124, 136f, 142, 148,
    153, 157
connectedness 111, 156
connection, emotional 111
consent 16, 25, 51–4, 119–30
context 12, 25, 51–4, 64–6, 91f, 96,
    144–8
contradictions 61, 78, 94f, 98f, 149
controversy 39, 152
Covid-19 70, 164–74
critique 4, 25f, 35, 82, 126,
    132–40, 142; ideological
    critique 35
cross-media 4, 6–18, 92f
cultural circuit 23f, 91
cultural consumption (and media
    consumption) 10, 11, 16, 66,
    67, 68, 98, 144
cultural knowledge 13, 60, 90, 94,
    115, 144, 186
cultural racism 153
culture: shared culture 15, 19

data: analysis 35–49, 121–6; collection 35–49, 63, 86, 121–3, 136f, 168; gathering 35f, 147; reduction 28, 119–22; scraping 41, 119–30
deconstruction 19–21
deductive approach 43, 153
diary *see* media diary
discourse 25, 29f, 62, 105–18, 141–51
distinction 9, 26, 124, 142f, 167
diversity 61, 175–87

emotion 23, 26, 43, 52, 83, 98, 106, 111–18, 122, 126, 133–8, 153f
empirical cycle 37
encoding/decoding 78
ethics 51–4
ethnicity 19, 21, 70, 96, 152–63, 178
ethnography 51–65, 84, 87–9, 154–64; archival ethnography 58; media ethnography 4, 7, 11–13, 38; netnography 38f, 55, 57–61; sensory ethnography 30, 83, 85–7, 155
everyday meaning making 185
experience 23, 48, 82–7, 110–14

fan 52, 59, 105–18, 131–40, 155, 159–61, 188f; acafan 137–9; fan practices 135
fandom 59, 108, 116, 131–40, 153, 155
fantasy 43, 48, 99
feeling 23–6, 110f, 148, 152f, 157–9, 178
flow 9
focus group 55–8, 152–63
frame 4, 16, 29, 30, 105–18
freedom 25f

gender 19, 21, 26, 27, 29, 38–9, 52, 73, 81, 95f, 120, 127, 153, 157, 186
genre(s) 11, 41, 109, 110, 118, 124, 125, 136, 137, 140, 144, 152
governmentality 21, 100, 167f
grounded theory 12, 28, 119, 156, 158

humor 54, 116, 129, 142–51, 165–73, 182–4

idealization 48
identification 64, 83, 108, 112, 113, 141, 158, 159
identity/ties 3, 9, 14f, 23f, 38f, 59–62, 64–72, 81f, 111, 120–30, 138, 152–8, 166, 181, 189
identity formation 24
ideology 20–5, 165
inductive approach 43, 152
informant 30
interpretative frame *see* frame
intersectionality 125, 175, 185
interview 55–8, 70–5; long interview 55–8, 155, 175–87
interviewee 30
interviewer 22, 71f, 177
iteration 36, 82

labeling 44–8, 94
labor 25, 131–40
lifeworld 12, 100
literacy 186
lived reality 111–15
liveness 70, 154, 157
locality 12

masculinity 86, 109, 114–16, 129
meaning-making 6, 13f, 16, 19, 21, 23–30, 72, 77, 82, 100, 146, 189
media diary 61, 66–8
media discourse 55–8, 142–51
media discourse analysis *see* analysis
media mapping 64–6
media technology 15f
mediation 3, 189
medium 6–8, 11
method 6, 12–14
methodology 20f, 26–8
myth 20–23

narrative analysis *see* analysis
nation-state 15
'natural' 20, 21, 24, 97
neoliberalism 21, 165, 167, 172f
netnography *see* ethnography
norm 14, 24–7, 146, 148
nostalgia 29, 148, 172, 176

observation *see* participant observation

paradigmatic logic 14f
paradox 22, 55, 94, 96
participant 30, 51f, 55–8, 70–4
participant design 35–7
participant observation 27, 51,
    56–8, 157
participative method 154f
performance 23, 26, 92, 96, 122,
    153, 164
performativity 97
photo elicitation 58
pleasure(s) 21f, 25, 38, 98f, 105, 136,
    157f, 161, 176, 181; guilty
    22, 98
positionality 55, 62, 70, 78f, 86, 124f,
    133, 147, 188
post-television 10, 132, 140
power 4, 21, 23, 27, 38, 43, 79, 90,
    116, 142, 165, 173, 176
prototype 89
pseudonym 53, 61, 176
psychology 22, 36
public sphere 126, 144, 170

queer 27
questionnaire 10, 28, 30, 36f

racism 153, 157, 176
rationality 22, 153
reflexivity 27, 50, 65, 78, 87, 189;
    self-reflexivity 37–9, 165, 168
religion 19
repertoire 4, 29, 30f, 48f, 74,
    108, 187
representation 13–15, 24–5, 38, 43,
    58–62, 83, 97, 122, 150, 176,
    179–83, 189
research: qualitative research 4, 12f,
    28, 30, 36f, 71, 81, 90, 157;

quantitative research 22, 30,
    36, 71
resemblance 48
respondent 30, 52–4, 68
rituals 38, 159

saturation 40, 147, 156, 162
scraping *see* data scraping
semiotic analysis *see* analysis
sensorial appeal 83f
sexism 39, 145, 153
snowballing 55, 70, 167
solidarity 165, 167, 171f
stereotype(s) 25, 155, 184–6
storytelling 10–12, 19, 24, 28, 43,
    107, 159
streaming 8, 10, 65, 72, 79, 86, 108,
    134, 145
subject formation 111
subjectivity 4, 21f, 24, 27, 64
survey 22, 35f, 97
syntagmatic logic 14f

taste 16, 19, 22, 76, 100, 124, 127,
    142–9, 155, 157
thematic analysis *see* analysis
theorization 19, 36, 43, 90–101, 107
transcript 13, 28, 35, 44, 93f

viewer 30
viewing experience 10, 12, 60,
    124–6, 136
visual analysis *see* analysis
visual regime 176, 183

working through 66, 164–74
world view *see* ideology

zeitgeist 108

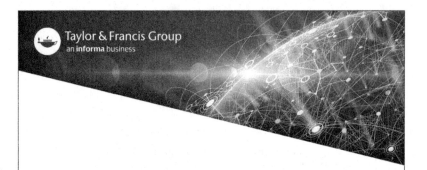

Printed in the United States
by Baker & Taylor Publisher Services